Thanks for the Memories

Strom

DINING IN FRANCE

DINING IN
FRANCE

by Christian Millau

photographs by Philippe-Louis Houzé

Stoddart

Text copyright © 1986 Christian Millau.
Recipes © 1986 Stewart, Tabori & Chang, Inc.
Introduction copyright © 1986 Pierre Salinger.
All photographs copyright ©1986 Philippe-Louis
Houzé, except as noted below.
Page 166 ©1986 Barton & Guestier.
Page 82 ©1986 Gault Millau.
Pages 23 (two), 31, 41, 152, ©1986
Monica Douek.

Text translated by Sheila Mooney Mall.
Directed by André Gayot.
Recipes translated, tested, and adapted by
Harriet Reilly and Tina Ujlaki.
Captions by Elizabeth Powers.

Dining in France is based upon the Public
Television series created and produced by CEL
Communications, Inc. and Initial Groupe, directed by
Jean Louis Comolli, in association with KQED/Golden
Gate Productions, San Francisco and FR3, France.

First published in 1986 by
Stoddart Publishing Co. Limited
34 Lesmill Road
Don Mills, Toronto
Canada M3B 2T6

First published in the United States by
Stewart, Tabori & Chang, Inc.

Canadian Cataloguing in Publication Data

Millau, Christian.
Dining in France

Accompanies the television series, Dining in France.
Includes index.
ISBN 0-7737-2081-2

1. Cookery, French. 2. Restaurants, lunch rooms,
etc.—France. 3. Cooks—France.
4. France—Description and
travel—1975—I. Title.

TX637.M54 1986   647′.9544   C86-093156-0

Printed and bound in Italy

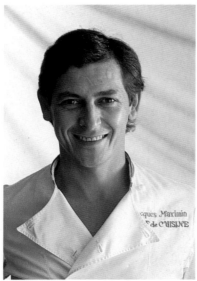

Jacques Maximin
Chantecler (Hôtel Negresco)

Georges Blanc

Jacques Chibois
Le Royal-Gray

CONTENTS

Alain Chapel

Michel Trama
L'Aubergade

Pierre Gagnaire
Saint-Etienne

INTRODUCTION by PIERRE SALINGER

GREAT CHEFS. FINE FOOD. Superb wines. Three-hundred-sixty-five different cheeses. Champagne, a bubbly wine that has become the symbol of celebration. Scores of regions, attached to their past and their differences from the rest of France. All these are elements that make up the extraordinary diversity and quality of dining in France.

When the idea was first proposed to me of doing a television series on the subject, I wanted to go further than just making a tour of the greatest restaurants in France. They are, of course, part of the story. But in order to understand dining in France, you also have to know something about its past, its present, and its future.

France is the birthplace and kingdom of gastronomy. From the days of the Greco-Roman empire, through the Middle Ages, the era of Kings, the French Revolution, the Empire, through until today, the evolution of French food and the manner in which it is presented has been striking. That evolution is linked to history and to families who have passed down special talents from generation to generation. We set out to do the series and this book at the same time and spent almost a year traveling around

Michel Rostang

Bernard Loiseau
Hôtel de la Côte d'Or

Louis Outhier
L'Oasis

France. We met the great chefs such as Pierre Troisgros, Paul Bocuse, Jacques Maximin, Georges Blanc, Roger Verge, and Alain Senderens. And through them we learned about their styles, about the way they choose their foods and wines, about their conceptions of cooking.

A real chef is a whole organization. Take Pierre Troisgros, who with his now deceased brother, Jean, founded a restaurant in the central French town of Roanne, just across the street from the railroad station. (The station is specially painted in pink and green to match one of the Troisgros specialties—Le Saumon à l'Oseille—salmon with sorell). Troisgros has a special producer for his cheeses, for his wines, for his special French Charolais beef. I was able to visit the Troisgros restaurant and hotel, and watch the smooth workings of a not-so-simple operation.

In Vonnas, the young Georges Blanc, who took over the restaurant La Mère Blanc from his mother when he was still in his twenties, took me to see how they raise the very special Bresse chicken; the raising of *poulet de bresse* is carefully controlled to produce high quality. In Nice, at the Hôtel Negresco, Jacques Maximin, an artist of desserts, taught me how chocolate can play a key role in a superb French meal. In

Reims, Gerard Boyer, now installed in the historic Château des Crayères, told me the history of Champagne, and how each brand is a blend of wines mixed to a certain taste. In Paris I visited Androuet, the most famous cheese dealer in France, and went through his incredible caves where almost all of France's three-hundred-sixty-five cheeses are prepared for sale or delivery to top restaurants. And to conclude the show I went to the second floor of the Eiffel Tower in Paris to the new haute cuisine restaurant, the Jules Verne—a combination of great food and an exceptional view of the city.

Our year of dining in France was a very special adventure that we attempt to communicate through television and in book form. This volume will be a valuable asset if you really want to know about dining in France.

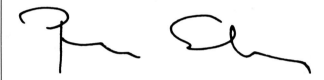

Pierre Salinger
Paris
February 1986

Gérard Boyer
Château des Crayères

Claude Deligne with
Jean-Claude Vrinat
Taillevent

Paul and Marc Haeberlin
Auberge de l'Ill

DINING IN FRANCE

ALL AROUND YOU THE furniture is mahogany with brass trim. Wisteria motifs cascade down stained-glass windows. Beveled mirrors, pink lamps, and Art Nouveau murals pull you back to the turn of the century as you sip Champagne at your table. The sommelier approaches and recommends some wines; you discuss your choice with him. Later your meal arrives: warm lobster in an aromatic broth, or perhaps roast pheasant.

A big mill stands near the house. Nearby, thick walls of green hide a delightful garden. After a day along the Riviera, you want to sample the "cuisine of the sun," Provençal cooking that freely uses aromatic herbs, local vegetables, and light sauces. You cannot resist the tiny red mullet with tomatoes and herb-scented olive oil . . . until the truffle-stuffed zucchini blossoms tempt you.

In a tiny village outside Beaune in Burgundy, in the shadow of a church steeple, you notice a vine-covered cottage. Outside are cats and dogs and chickens; inside are jam pots, pickle jars, and huge loaves of bread. There are tables, benches, and chairs for twenty people; there is

also glorious country cooking. You sample an exquisite crayfish terrine made from a seventeenth-century recipe. At dessert, you find the chocolate tart sublime.

The pleasures of dining in France are unequaled. The traditions that prevail today originated in the royal courts and were brought to a wider audience later, by restaurants that are now part of history. The art of French cooking has recently been renewed by nouvelle cuisine, and today, a younger generation of chefs is exploring even newer gastronomic directions. But the experience of dining remains essentially unchanged: the ambiance is elegant, the eating leisurely, the ingredients rare, and the meals are works of art.

French cooking, in fact, comprises several very different culinary styles. The diversity can be bewildering, and even many French people lack a clear idea of what "haute cuisine," "classic cuisine," "nouvelle cuisine," and "regional" or "bourgeois" cooking really are. It is worthwhile to explain what is meant by each term.

Grande cuisine, or *haute cuisine*, originated in the courts of the French kings. The first to have prided himself on his table was Charlemagne. Crowned emperor in 800 A.D., it was he who launched the fashion for eating peacock: the birds were brought to the table arrayed in

Among the 200,000 bottles of wine La Tour d'Argent has in its famous wine cellar are a Château Citran 1855, a Château d'Yquem 1871, and a Chambertin 1865. Chambertin, a Burgundy, was preferred by Napoleon.

their colorful plumage, fire spurting from their beaks. In medieval times, the royal kitchens employed hundreds of people to prepare an extremely elaborate cuisine rivaled only by the ornate dishes served in the halls of the greatest lords. The common folk generally ate simple and rather crude fare: soups, roasts, and the like.

The Renaissance marked the dawn of a new gastronomic era in France. When Catherine de Medici wed the Duke of Orleans (who later became Henry II of France) in 1533, she brought with her to the Louvre (then the royal residence) her own chefs, recipes, even ingredients and spices. The court's heavy and complicated cuisine gave way to simpler, more refined dishes; it was at this time that fish was first prepared in sauce.

French cuisine evolved over time, influenced by fashion and by the personal styles of succeeding sovereigns: Louis XIV (1638–1715), the Sun King, was a glutton; Louis XV (1710–1774) was a refined gourmet. Invariably, however, it was rich food expensively prepared and remained exclusively available to the privileged classes.

At the time of the French Revolution, restaurants began to emerge and French cuisine became available to the public. In the nineteenth century it entered the homes of aristocrats and wealthy bourgeois, all of whom had chefs or at least a cook and a kitchen staff. The most famous chefs cooked in private houses, like Carême, who is known as the Cook of kings and the King of cooks. He worked for Talleyrand, Napoleon's foreign minister, and for the Prince Regent in England. Today, although few French families employ kitchen staffs, grande cuisine is available to anyone in restaurants, with only the prices protecting its exclusive status.

The grande cuisine of the nineteenth and first half of the twentieth century is known as *classic cuisine*. A cookbook by the famed chef Auguste Escoffier, which was published early in this century, defined the classic method in detail and remained a bible for chefs for decades. But by the 1960s, classic cuisine had entered a period of decline. Taste was sacrificed to appearance. Rich and costly ingredients, such as foie gras, caviar, and truffles, were ubiquitous. Bad habits—leaving stock pots long on the back burner, preparing dishes in advance and reheating them—were common, and France's gastronomic reputation became sadly tarnished. Some restaurants survived solely on past glories and prepared food the way they did fifty years ago, such as Point in Vienne, not far from Lyons, or Le Père Bise in Talloires on the Lac d'Annecy, to mention only the most famous.

Most classic grande cuisine preparations have by now vanished from the menus of renowned restaurants: in truth, the dogmatic classic cuisine was generally better to look at than to eat. *Nouvelle cuisine* is an approach to cooking that emerged at the beginning of the 1970s in reaction to classic cuisine. It freed the creative inspiration of young chefs who had felt bound by Escoffier's rules. Within fifteen years, its guiding principles became part of the French culinary heritage, and they continue to inspire the best dishes in the best restaurants.

Nouvelle cuisine advocated a few simple practices that seemed to correspond to changing tastes. People began to demand lighter food in keeping with their concern for health and fitness. There was a trend toward simplicity and the use of fresh products and seasonal ingredients; shortened cooking times allowed vegetables and fish to retain their natural flavors and nutrients. Lightness became the new watchword, with alcohol, flour, butter, cream, and fat avoided entirely or kept at a minimum.

Menus grew smaller, which meant restaurants no longer had to keep stocks of unused food in the refrigerator. The menus also changed often, to make use of seasonal products and reflect the chef's latest inspiration. This new emphasis on personal artistry encouraged experiments and welcomed influences from regional cooking and from abroad—particularly from Asian cuisine. New kitchen technologies, such as food processors and microwave ovens, were adopted as well.

The look of dining itself changed. Large plates, called "American plates" in France, allowed chefs to arrange food in an appetizing way and avoid unintentional mixtures. The philosophy of nouvelle cuisine is that the experience of dining should be totally pleasurable, with the presentation of the food and refinement of the table setting complementing the quality and sophistication of the cuisine.

Regional, or *rustic*, *cooking* includes many centuries-old traditions. In France, every sixty miles produces a new region with not only its own architecture and landscape but also its own cooking. The richness and diversity of regional cooking give the French a fantastically complex culinary heritage. Yet because the modern world tends to reduce this diversity, most people today eat the same kind of food whether they live in Provence or Brittany. Restaurants have become the preservers of culinary traditions and nowadays there is a significant trend toward a return to regional roots. Although some restaurateurs on the Riviera, for instance, serve canned fish soup, and some in Alsace serve little but sauerkraut, more and more restaurants are searching out forgotten local recipes and offering a gastronomic panorama of their region. Nearly all French regional specialties can be had in Paris, but the best place to sample them is on their home turf where the finest products are grown and local cooks prepare them.

In Paris, *bistro cuisine* is also called *cuisine bourgeoise* because it is the kind of cooking people would traditionally eat every day. Because it consists chiefly of long-simmered dishes requiring a good deal of time to prepare, bourgeois cooking these days is less often to be found in the home than in little restaurants. It is generous fare, sometimes a bit heavy, but perfectly delicious when made well. The most well known bourgeois specialties are dishes like pot-au-feu (boiled beef), navarin d'agneau (lamb stew), daube de boeuf (beef stew), hachis Parmentier (meat and potato hash), tête de veau sauce gribiche (calf's head with a mayonnaise sauce), boeuf mode (beef stew), stuffed cabbage, leg of lamb with garlic, grilled pig's trotters, lapin chasseur (rabbit with tomato and mushroom sauce), mouton aux haricots blancs (mutton stew with white beans), raie au beurre noir or noisette (skate with browned butter), and grilled sole. An excellent lamb stew is in fact served to the staff at Lasserre, although it is not considered elegant enough to be listed on the menu!

19

The famous, rich ingredients of French grande cuisine were all once produced in France, but the industrialization of the countryside has meant that many types of produce have died out or become scarce. Once exclusively French products now come from all over the world.

The famed "Périgord truffles" have almost totally vanished from Périgord, in the department of Dordogne, although they are unearthed in the neighboring Lot region and more often still in the department of Vaucluse, in the Rhône Valley. Today's truffle crop is four times smaller than at the turn of the century, while demand keeps growing. Nearly fifty percent of the French truffle production is in fact Spanish. And since they are absolutely indistinguishable, truffles from across the border are quite legally labeled Périgord truffles.

Frogs have become so raré that most served in restaurants are imports from Poland, Turkey, Yugoslavia, or Bangladesh. Most of the famed "Burgundy snails" come from Eastern Europe. Foie gras is so much in demand that small French farms cannot raise fatted geese fast enough; almost half of the foie gras canned in France originates in Bulgaria, Israel, or Hungary. Crayfish are imported from Poland and Yugoslavia, pigs from East Germany and China, tomatoes from the Netherlands, green beans from Senegal, lobsters from South Africa. But if people are ready to pay the price and to go to a bit of trouble, it is still possible to find ingredients of French origin. In fact, the level of quality has risen in a pretty spectacular way.

Manners and customs in France are not so different from those in English-speaking countries, but subtle differences do exist. Dinner is later and more leisurely, for example, and dress is generally more formal. Restaurant personnel—especially the head waiter and sommelier—are members of a professional elite, and their advice should be respected, though it need not be followed. Familiarity with a few French traditions will ensure a memorable dining experience.

Reservations. One must make dinner reservations far in advance at the more celebrated restaurants in Paris and from May to December in the top provincial establishments. Many restaurants have grown wary of reservations from abroad; too many customers have forgotten to cancel their reservations and simply not shown up, leaving the restaurants with an empty table for the evening. Sending a check for about fifty dollars with a letter or making a credit card deposit through a travel agent, however, will

20

generally guarantee a table. A risky alternative would be to call a restaurant after 9 p.m. to see if a no-show or last-minute cancellation has left a table free.

If top restaurants are full, consult a guidebook that reviews restaurants or ask the hotel concierge for a recommendation. In less celebrated restaurants it is usually possible to reserve in the morning for that or the following evening. For those with no time at all to make reservations, there is usually room to squeeze in at a brasserie, where reservations are not needed. In the country, a guidebook is still the traveler's best bet, though a local grocer, baker, butcher, or cheesemonger will often provide the name of his favorite restaurant. In general, tables are easier to find in provincial restaurants, which are more spacious than their Parisian counterparts.

Dinner normally begins at 8 p.m., although some restaurants serve as early as 7:30. People rarely appear in "les grands restaurants" before 9 p.m., and in the more fashionable spots Parisians have taken to dining later and later. Most of the great French restaurants have only one sitting, and leisure at table is expected. Having arrived at 9 p.m., you may still be seated at midnight, and no one will hurry you.

Dining at lunchtime. Although evening is unquestionably the best time to visit a great restaurant, some of the most celebrated establishments, such as Maxim's, Lucas-Carton, La Tour d'Argent, Jules Verne, Laurent, Le Divellec, Le Carré des Feuillants, or a top-drawer bistro like L'Ami Louis, are enjoyable at lunch. Provincial restaurants worth an afternoon visit are La Côte Saint-Jacques, Gérard Boyer, Lameloise, Léon de Lyon, Pic, and L'Auberge des Templiers. Plan to arrive between 12:30 and 2 p.m. for a lunchtime meal.

How to dress. A jacket and tie are appropriate for men at most Parisian restaurants; women should avoid pantsuits. While the French are far less formal than in the past, questions of dress are still not taken lightly in luxury restaurants. The only place in Paris where black tie is obligatory is Maxim's, on Friday night.

What to order. In any of the top restaurants, let the head waiter make a few suggestions before ordering (it is likely he will speak English). His job is to know how to harmonize a succession of flavors. If a dish does not meet your expectations, do not hesitate to send it back; any fine restaurant will immediately change it.

Although gourmet restaurants in the provinces have traditionally offered commendable fixed-price meals to their customers, Parisian establishments long deemed this practice inelegant. Lately, however, they have taken a different view, and, in the interest of filling their dining rooms at lunch, many now offer very attractive fixed-price menus that are far less costly than ordering à la carte. Interesting lunches are offered at La Tour d'Argent, Robuchon, Le Grand Véfour, Jules Verne, Le Bourdonnais, Jacques Cagna, La Pactole, Duquesnoy, Faugeron, Beauvilliers, Morot-Gaudry, Le Divellec, and Vivarois. The sampling menu, or menu-dégustation, which provides small portions of six or eight dishes, was launched about fifteen years ago by Troisgros in Roanne. Today, a good many other restaurants have adopted the sampling system, which offers an excellent way of getting to know a restaurant's specialties.

A small- or medium-sized restaurant almost always offers one or more daily specials. They are good choices because they are likely to be made with fresh ingredients.

Despite the mystique of truffles, they are simply underground mushrooms with a heavenly scent. The deep black ones preserved in Cognac are likely to be real Périgord truffles.

Foie gras, lobster, scallops, prawns, sweetbreads, or game may be listed on the menus of small restaurants with no particular reputation, but they are likely to be of mediocre quality. The best advice is to eat such grande cuisine only in great restaurants; elsewhere, stick to bourgeois cooking. Select something simple instead: an omelet, pot-au-feu, or a lamb stew. They are bound to be better choices.

Ask the head waiter or the owner if the dish you wish to order is in season. There is a world of difference between fresh green beans or prawns and frozen ones. And fish tends to be fresh on Friday because that is when demand is at its peak. Monday's fish is bound to have spent three days in the refrigerator. Most seafood restaurants, in fact, are closed on Monday.

What to drink. Most of the great restaurants have at least one wine steward, or sommelier. The sommelier is a revered figure in French restaurants; the secrets of the trade take a lifetime to learn. His (or her) job is to advise the diner. First listen to what he recommends, then study the wine list. Check the prices before ordering, but remember that it is not the sommelier's aim to push expensive bottles. France produces literally hundreds of thousands of unique wines, so the expert advice of the sommelier should be welcomed.

Some sommeliers taste the wine first, others have the diner taste it. If you find fault with the wine, point it out at the tasting; the restaurant will change it immediately. This does not apply if the bottle is very old: one orders a Lafite-Rothschild 1903 or a Latour 1870 at one's own risk. If the wine is undrinkable, you can at least save the bottle. If a wine does not suit you although there is nothing wrong with it, you will be expected to pay for it.

Some bistros and a few restaurants offer a house wine. It is never a great wine, but it is usually good and reasonably priced. For those who do not drink alcohol, most restaurants serve good brands of mineral water. It is best to avoid cola, milk, hard liquor, and rosé wine. Hard liquor, by the way, tends to dull the palate, so before eating try a glass of Champagne, wine, or a kir (wine with black currant liqueur) instead.

Tipping. In many restaurants, the menu prices include the service charge. Others automatically add a charge of 12 percent, 15 percent, or 18 percent to the tab. One is not obliged to leave an additional tip; but if the service was particularly good, something extra can be left for the wine steward—10 or 20 francs on a 200- or 300-franc wine bill—and for the head waiter.

Clockwise from top left: Jean-Marie Amat's restaurant, located in a large white stone villa in Bordeaux, offers elegant regional cuisine. In Cannes, the Carlton remains a monument to the past luxury of grand hotels. The glass ceiling in Bofinger, one of Paris' oldest and most attractive restaurants, is decorated with flowers and fruit motifs. Michel Guerard's meals at the restaurant-inn Eugénie-les-Bains may encourage you to spend more time in southwestern France than you had planned.

THE HISTORIC FRENCH RESTAURANTS

Chapter

2

BEFORE THE FRENCH REVolution in 1789 the restaurant as we know it did not exist. Inns served a single menu at given hours for a fixed price; from the time of Louis XIV, the keepers of eating houses were authorized to serve three (but no more) different meat dishes in their shops; wine merchants could serve food too, though again the number of dishes was strictly limited. Thus, opportunities for lunching or dining out were few, and one assumes there was likewise a small, monotonous selection of soups, porridges, vegetables, cheeses, and fruits. "Nearly everyone believes," wrote a German writer by the name of Nemeitz in 1718, "that one dines well in France, particularly in Paris; that view is mistaken."

"Grande cuisine," the basis of French gastronomic fame, did exist, but it was the exclusive privilege of a small minority. The king and his court were served by the best cooks of the realm, who from medieval times had cultivated a brilliant, sophisticated, and costly culinary art, accompanied by opulent presentations. The nobles who formed the royal entourage also attached great importance to the pleasures of the table and vied with one another to obtain the best chefs. By the eighteenth century, the rich bourgeoisie, whose social and economic importance was increasing apace, presided at tables that reflected their ambition and wealth. Yet there was no public establishment where one could sample similarly refined fare.

After the Bastille had fallen, when the sinister guillotine performed its terrible office at what is now the Place de la Concorde, members of the nobility and the rich bourgeoisie either were imprisoned or had emigrated to Germany or England. Their cooks thus found themselves suddenly unemployed; several of those who had amassed considerable savings took it into their heads to open their own establishments and offer the same luxurious cuisine they had prepared for their former patrons to anyone who could afford to pay the price.

The most famous of these was Antoine Beauvilliers, who had been chef to Louis XVI's brother, the Comte de Provence. Beauvilliers opened a "restaurant" (the word originally signified a "fortifying broth," or restorative) at Palais-Royal, a fashionable Parisian address that also abounded in prostitutes. Wearing a sword at his side, Beauvilliers, with a studiedly regal step, paced up and down his dining rooms where customers fed on delicate fare served in silver dish-

It is said that one dines on dreams at Maxim's. From its earliest days to the present, Maxim's has been the place to go to be seen.

es. Thus was the modern restaurant born. Paradoxically, its popularity continued to grow throughout the revolutionary period, despite the Reign of Terror in 1794, and despite the food shortages that forced most ordinary people to go hungry. On the day that Marie Antoinette was guillotined, the jury that had condemned her gathered in the private dining room of a restaurant on the rue de Rivoli (at the spot where the Hôtel Meurice now stands) to partake of foie gras, woodcocks, gratinéed quail, sweetbreads, and truffle-stuffed hens, all washed down with Sauternes and Champagne. After the Revolution, during the Directoire (1795–1799) and later under Napoleon, restaurants were still the rage; Palais-Royal had by then become a gastronomic mecca, and establishments like Le Grand Véfour and Véry drew pilgrims from the world over. Later, when Napoleon III (1852–1870) ascended the throne, the restaurant scene shifted to the neighborhood of the Opéra on the prestigious new boulevards constructed by Baron Haussmann.

There, until World War II, the most brilliant chapter in the history of Parisian gastronomy unfolded, in restaurants like the Café Anglais, the Café Riche, Tortoni, Larue, Voisin, Paillard, or La Maison Dorée.

Few traces remain of that era. One after the other, the restaurants vanished as the times and the world around them changed. Since World War II, formerly splendid restaurants were often in a sorry state. Repairs were usually too costly, and the atmosphere in restaurants had become dismal to Parisians craving gaiety, warmth, and vibrancy after the long wartime of sadness and deprivation. When the Café de Paris closed its doors in 1953 after serving a final meal to the celebrated writer André Malraux, its kitchen and dining room staff was still

huge. But customers had changed: their tastes had become less elaborate, their appetites more moderate. Gone were the days when a trencherman like Honoré de Balzac would sit down to table at Véry's and wolf down a hundred oysters, twelve lamb chops, a duckling with turnips, a brace of roast partridges, a whopping sole in cream sauce, assorted desserts, and a dozen pears! Nor could one witness the spectacle of three Parisian gentlemen at the Café Anglais, which closed its doors in 1913, spending a small fortune—the equivalent of $5,000 today—for a feast that consisted of a hundred pairs of frogs' legs. (The rivers and swamps around Paris had frozen over that year, so the restaurant's owner had been obliged to hire fifty workers to break through the ice and catch the creatures.)

Not too many years ago, it indeed appeared that the final knell had tolled for most of the grand old monuments of the Parisian restaurant trade. But then, to everyone's surprise, some began to give signs of new life: a number of historic eateries not only revived, but burst back with new vigor. Maxim's and La Tour d'Argent had continued to be glittering exceptions to the general demise, though a few years back people were starting to doubt that those two venerable institutions would survive the century. Now each has tables booked for New Year's Eve, 1999!

Founded in 1893, Maxim's was absolutely the place to be seen at the time of the World's Fair, held in Paris in 1900. Celebrated figures from the world of finance, the arts, and show business all gathered to carouse there amid the mad and magical Art Nouveau decor, a veritable forest of mahogany trimmed in brass and bronze. Extravagances were not only permitted, they were positively encouraged. One evening, a cotton magnate by the name of MacFadden had a nude

Today's patrons enjoy the same splendor as when Maxim's was host to the reigning heads of Europe. Its Art Nouveau interior has recently been restored by Pierre Cardin.

woman carried to his table on a silver platter; another eccentric made his entrance on a horse; and Ivan, the Grand Duke of Russia, finished eight bottles of Mumm Champagne, then sank to the floor in a stupor. World War I put an end to such follies; during the 1930s, Maxim's was simply the most elegant restaurant in Paris, perhaps in the world. During the Occupation, German officers merrily quaffed Maxim's Champagne. In the 1960s and 70s, after an eclipse, Maxim's recovered its prestige. On a given evening, seated side by side on what was dubbed the "Royal Banquette" (five tables numbered 16 to 20), current royalty could be seen: Jackie Onassis and Maria Callas, the Duke and Duchess of Windsor, the Maharani of Baroda dripping with diamonds, and Grace and Rainier of Monaco. Albert, the portly director, seated his guests according to their wealth or celebrity; newcomers were greeted with an icy glance that could cow the stoutest heart. But gradually, the movers and shakers dropped in less frequently or else vanished altogether and the customary Friday black-tie dinners fell into disuse.

In the early 1980s, Louis Vaudable, who had owned Maxim's for almost half a century, decided to retire. Who would take on this endangered monument, with its staff of 110 employees, its 200,000-bottle wine cellar, its huge operating expenses, and its outdated kitchens? Pierre Cardin, already a stockholder in the restaurant, was an unlikely savior. The famous couturier took over Maxim's partly for the fun of it, and partly to give Paris a new sense of festivity. The first thing he did was to have it cleaned. (Paul Bocuse, who once worked in Maxim's kitchens, swears that he used to chase rats there!) At the sumptuous reopening gala in 1982, Cardin's guests discovered a newly resplendent Maxim's. In the large ground-floor dining room, which featured an orchestra and the famous Royal Banquette, the glass roof and famous murals had recovered their former color and luminosity. The first-floor dining room and bar, "L'Impériale," had been entirely redone with Art Nouveau period furniture. The second-floor salons, used for receptions, cocktail parties, and private dinners, were redecorated with

extraordinary attention to detail: a mahogany bar, stained glass windows with wisteria motifs, polychromed cornices, beveled mirrors, pink lamps, and wall murals.

Overnight, Maxim's once again became a beacon in the nightlife of Paris. Evening dress is now de rigueur on Fridays, and Pierre Cardin often throws elaborate parties to honor his friends from the worlds of opera, dance, film, or art. Lunch hour at Maxim's is no longer deserted; midday meals in the Garden Room—a kind of conservatory, with a glass wall that affords a view of the Rue Royale—are among the liveliest in Paris. A dinner table in the Grande Salle, beneath the glass roof, must be reserved at least a week in advance. Celebrities are seated, naturally, on the Royal Banquette; the less-well-known are directed to the left side; the rest to the right and the middle of the room in front of the orchestra. A six-piece band plays current hits in a style that makes rock and roll sound like Viennese waltzes.

Probably no other restaurant in France serves

more Champagne than Maxim's. An ice bucket with a bottle of bubbly is automatically placed on every table, though should diners prefer another type of wine, the cellar holds all the best growths (some at staggering prices) as well as modest wines at fairly reasonable prices. Maxim's food has never been its drawing card. Although chef Michel Menant has lots of talent (on advance order, he can prepare exquisite meals), the eclectic menu jumbles together elaborate, outmoded "haute cuisine" (saddle of veal Orloff, pheasant Souvaroff), bourgeois-style cooking (beef in aspic), and other dishes of more modern inspiration (not always the most successful), which gives the cuisine here a somewhat heterogeneous air. It is wise to choose the simplest offerings, like the marvelous warm lobster à la nage, in aromatic broth. Maxim's frequently serves almost five hundred meals a day, but with a staff that includes ten head waiters, fourteen waiters, seventeen busboys, and six wine stewards, service is swift and precise. The new young director, Jean-Pierre Guevel, unlike the notorious Albert, greets every guest with the same warm smile.

La Tour d'Argent is definitely the oldest restaurant in Paris. Founded in 1582, it is said that forks first appeared at table here. For years, owner Claude Terrail, who with his boutonniere and London-tailored suits cuts a dashing figure, steadfastly refused to consider any changes in the food served at La Tour d'Argent. Apparently persuaded that his cuisine was the best in the world, he did not see the need to renew his menu (a handsome piece of work, by the way, with a sumptuous silver cover), which offered dishes that were so rich and so complicated that one sometimes wondered exactly what was on the plate. But when he finally realized that his restaurant was in peril of being permanently out-

Although Dominique Bouchet has presided over a culinary revolution at La Tour d'Argent, he has not removed the restaurant's famous numbered duck from the menu..

stripped by its competitors, he gave carte blanche to his young chef, Dominique Bouchet. Bouchet has accomplished a veritable revolution at La Tour d'Argent.

Most of the pompous preparations wallowing in rich sauces have been replaced by a delicate, refined cuisine that produces marvels like the pâté of lobster in truffle aspic, sautéed langoustines and artichokes seasoned with hazelnut oil, roast salmon with beef marrow, a remarkable leg of lamb braised for several hours with vegetables and then served with a spoon. Bouchet's masterpiece is an old recipe he unearthed: very rare duck breast plunged into boiling, highly spiced broth accompanied by souffléed potatoes.

The tidal wave that swept the menu did spare the famous "duck Tour d'Argent," known throughout the world for almost a century. It was around 1890 that Frédéric, former head waiter and later owner of the restaurant, was inspired to serve a duck in two separate courses: first the breast, covered with a sauce thickened with the animal's blood; afterward the broiled duck's legs. The true stroke of genius was numbering the ducks and giving each client a card bearing the bird's number. In 1900, Grand Duke Vladimir of Russia consumed duck number 6,043 and on May 16, 1948 Queen Elizabeth dined on number 185,387. In 1986, the total approaches 700,000!

In the 1930s, André Terrail, Claude's father, moved the restaurant from the ground floor to the building's top story, where it is today. The view that the restaurant affords of the Seine and, at night, of Notre Dame bathed in light, draws cries of delight and admiration from first-time patrons; one must reserve fairly far in advance to obtain a table near the picture window. On the ground floor, in the restaurant's former precincts, where the superb original wood panels remain, Claude Terrail exhibits historical memorabilia relating to the restaurant. Diners can inspect this interesting collection and sip an aperitif before entering the elevator that will take them to the top of La Tour. In the display cases are table and kitchen utensils (a sixteenth-century fork, a seventeenth-century coffee mill, a drinking glass that belonged to Empress Elizabeth I of Russia), a superb collection of antique menus, and autographs of famous patrons from President Eisenhower to the present Emperor of Japan. Most impressive is the table at which the "Three Emperors' Dinner" took place on June 7, 1867; it is laid with the same cloth and dishes today. The three were Alexander II, the czar of Russia; the czarevitch Alexander; and William II of Prussia.

To finish the evening, tradition dictates that patrons of La Tour d'Argent descend to the wine cellar for a glass of old Cognac or Armagnac. Nearly 200,000 bottles sleep in the cellar just a few yards from the Seine river bed. These imposing surroundings are the setting for a "sound and light show," narrated by Claude Terrail. A spotlight illuminates in turn each of the most precious bottles in the collection: a Château Citran 1855, a Château d'Yquem 1871, a Chambertin 1865, a Cognac Fine Champagne 1797. Just before World War II, the millionaire Pierpont Morgan had a couple of James Bond types spirit away two bottles of Napoleon Cognac from La Tour d'Argent wine cellar. Although he had offered Terrail a small fortune, the American had not succeeded in persuading him to part with the brandy. In their place, Terrail found a letter of apology and a blank check. A good sport, he returned the check to Pierpont Morgan, who kept the bottles.

Of all the restaurants that flourished around

the gardens of the Palais-Royal during the Revolution and under Napoleon, only one still stands today, but it is unquestionably one of the loveliest in the world: Le Grand Véfour. In the darkest days of the Terror, Le Grand Véfour was a favorite meeting place for counterrevolutionaries. Later, young General Bonaparte was a regular customer, and until the end of the nineteenth century all the celebrities of the day dined there, from the great gastronome Brillat-Savarin to Victor Hugo. Then decline set in, and the place became just another dingy neighborhood café. But in the 1950s, a chef from Bordeaux named Raymond Oliver restored some of its former splendor to Le Grand Véfour. Jean Cocteau and Colette, who lived a few steps away, ate there frequently; soon Le Grand Véfour was again a fashionable spot. Thanks to a weekly television cooking show, Raymond Oliver found himself the most famous chef in France, beating even Paul Bocuse in the polls. Like the latter, Oliver took to spending less and less time in his kitchen, cooking virtually only for the camera. By the 1960s the gastronomic reputation of Le Grand Véfour declined, and the restaurant's decor deteriorated at a truly alarming rate. Struck down by illness, Raymond Oliver decided to sell Le Grand Véfour. He had the good fortune to meet up with Jean Taittinger (of the Champagne and the Concorde hotel chain group), who already owned the Hôtel de Crillon and had a great interest in historical sites. Taittinger completely restored the restaurant's glorious original decor, including its painted ceiling and the allegorical murals under glass that date from the reign of Napoleon III.

The atmosphere, at once lively and refined, makes for enchanting luncheons and dinners. A new chef has injected fresh vigor into the cooking as well. André Signoret overhauled and renewed Le Grand Véfour's repertory. Although not an out-and-out modernist, he serves a light cuisine that immediately lured back the chic Parisian clientele. The food is very good (salt cod with celery and bay, bass with mustard garnished with french-fried fennel, filet of lamb in a potato cake, veal kidney and sweetbreads with lemon) and served in so exceptional a setting that one easily sees why Le Grand Véfour has had such rousing success.

Before we leave the Taittinger family, we should say a few words about the Crillon. The hotel's restaurant is also, in its way, a historical monument. Its reputation is fairly recent, for a few years ago the hotel had only a grill room. It was decided to convert one of the large salons into a dining room called Les Ambassadeurs. With its marble and trompe l'oeil decorations, the room is a masterpiece, the work of the architect Jacques Gabriel who, under Louis XV, designed and built the Place de la Concorde and the palaces that surround it. The excellent chef, Jean-Paul Bonin, is an advocate of light, modern, inventive cuisine (tomato-stuffed red mullet steamed with basil, prawns in aspic with cabbage, truffled lobster, honeyed lamb with zucchini au gratin, numerous and particularly luscious desserts).

The Hôtel Ritz, another historic survivor, enjoyed a world-wide gastronomic reputation early in the century thanks to the celebrated chef, Auguste Escoffier. That reputation is now extinct, however, for the Ritz clings resolutely to its old-fashioned luxury hotel cuisine, which bears no comparison with the food served at the Crillon. Yet the new dining room that opens onto an indoor garden is a big hit with the customers: there will always be a public for the luxurious establishments that we once thought were a dying breed.

Jean-Paul Bonin orchestrates the kitchen of Les Ambassadeurs, the Hôtel Crillon.

Lucas-Carton is another case in point. The restaurant was saved in the nick of time by the owner of Rémy Martin Cognac and Krug Champagne. Already well known in the previous century, around 1900 Lucas-Carton was a favorite with political personalities and financial wheeler-dealers, who downed epic meals in its Belle Epoque dining room (which is now a historical monument). Afterward, those very grave messieurs would climb discreetly to the small private rooms on the upper floor, to tipple Champagne in far more amusing company.

It was over a luncheon at Lucas-Carton on November 10, 1918, that Foch, Joffre, Pershing, and French fixed the hour of the Armistice for the following day. Years later, Churchill often dropped in to sample the Lucas-Carton house specialty, woodcock with foie gras flamed in Cognac. After World War II, Lucas-Carton was still a great house. The chef in those days was a remarkable man named Mars Soustelle who had trained the then-obscure cooks named Paul Bocuse, Jean Troisgros, and Alain Senderens. In the 1960s Lucas-Carton was among the capital's foremost restaurants. The cream of Parisian society flocked to this address on the Place de la Madeleine. In his fabulously rich wine cellar, owner Alex Allegrier used to host extraordinary candlelight dinners for his friends, and serve such marvels as Romanée-Conti 1937 and Chartreuse 1900. After the death of chef Soustelle, the restaurant's cuisine went downhill When the sale of Lucas-Carton was confirmed in early 1985, only a very few former patrons still frequented the dusty dining room.

The sale, in fact, had almost fallen through. When the Allegrier family learned that the buyer intended to establish Alain Senderens at Lucas-Carton, they vetoed the deal: it was unthinkable to them that a former employee should be master at Lucas-Carton! In the end, though, the sale went through. The renovation work was finished in a few months' time, and Senderens threw open the doors of an entirely restored restaurant, again one of the most beautiful in Paris: warm blond wood, comfortable banquette seating, seductively soft lighting, and the small first-floor salons in fresh new colors. The pleasure one feels at Senderens' table is unalloyed; the sense of well-being that comes of dining in handsome surroundings intensifies the delights of a cuisine that is surely one of today's most creative. Ironically, the moment Senderens took over and revived the kitchens at Lucas-Carton, the sophisticates who had rarely poked their elegant noses into his former restaurant (the small L'Archestrate on the Left Bank) clamored for reservations at Senderens' new venue.

It is necessary to reserve a table at Lucas-Carton at least two weeks in advance. Neither of the two adjoining rooms has any particular advantage over the other; nor are there "good" or "bad" tables. Normally, it is Alain Senderens' wife, Eventhia, attractive, elegant, and just a bit shy, who welcomes diners at the door; but sometimes that duty devolves to the head waiter or even the cloakroom attendant. This occasional lapse in the quality of the reception is undeniably a weak point. However, the large and highly professional staff provides faultless service, devoid of needless ceremony or flourishes.

The food, with its bold, daring flavors, is not always understood by first-time diners, but the menu is catholic enough to suit most tastes. For example, for those who cannot stand "nouvelle cuisine," the menu offers one of the best ribs of beef to be found in Paris. Senderens garnishes it with wonderful deep-fried potato skins. But it would be a shame to neglect such delights as the millefeuille of duck liver with celery and apples, the bay scallop ravioli with zucchini, the lightly smoked poached salmon with asparagus, boned pigeon served with a ragoût of bell peppers, spiny lobster with leeks, sweetbreads with wild mushrooms, or the canard Apicius (roasted duck with honey). Determined to make good food healthful as well, Senderens has banished sauces from his repertory, usually replacing them with cooking juices or vegetable-based liaisons. Although he hasn't managed to eliminate fat entirely, he never adds a single unnecessary gram to his dishes; hence the delicacy of his cuisine, which lets you rise from the table with a light stomach.

The wine cellar is exceedingly well stocked. In 1985, a customer from California shelled out $6,000 . . . just for the wine bill! His table of eight had ordered some of the greatest vintages of the century: Château d'Yquem 1947, Lafite-Rothschild 1945, and Petrus 1953.

Taillevent, located in a little street near the Champs-Elysées, cannot boast as long a history as Lucas-Carton, yet the restaurant is a monument nonetheless. Founded just after the last war by André Vrinat, Taillevent is located in a private mansion that once belonged to the Duc de Morny, half-brother of Napoleon III. (The

restaurant's name recalls France's first chef, Guillaume Tirel, known as Taillevent. Besides serving as head cook from 1368 to 1371 to Charles VI, he compiled a cookbook, called *Le Viandier*.) For a while the restaurant was celebrated chiefly for the riches of its wine cellar: 130,000 bottles, including such collectors' items as a Romanée-Conti 1899, a Château d'Yquem 1869, and a Lafite-Rothschild 1806.

Taillevent would undoubtedly have aged just as sedately as Lasserre, a restaurant that appeared on the Parisian scene at about the same time, and suffered the same—relative—eclipse, had André Vrinat not turned the restaurant over to his son, Jean-Claude, in 1975. The latter infused new blood into the enterprise and quickly made it one of the finest restaurants in France. Jean-Claude Vrinat had no particular vocation for the restaurant business; in fact, he had no special knowledge of food. He had just graduated from the Institut des Hautes Etudes Commerciales (the French equivalent of the Harvard Business School) when his father asked

The luxurious Art Nouveau interior at Lucas-Carton in Paris was designed by Louis Majorelle.

him to come to work at Taillevent. Although he did not become a chef himself, Jean-Claude threw himself into his job with so great a passion that he totally transformed Taillevent's ultra-classic style. He sent chef Claude Deligne to training stints with the Troisgros brothers in Roanne (near Lyons), and with Fredy Girardet in Switzerland; today, Vrinat is still involved in the creation of every new dish served in his restaurant. Such professionalism explains the success of Taillevent, one of the rare great restaurants in France where the owner is not also the chef. A modest man—he considers Joël Robuchon's cuisine superior to that of his own restaurant—Vrinat pays painstaking attention to every detail; he surely merits the title "premier restaurateur of France."

Tables must be reserved several weeks in advance at Taillevent—especially for the evening. Tables are laid in three connecting rooms; never more than one hundred guests are served in a single evening so that service is impeccable. The decor is sober but very elegant, with carved paneling, old paintings, and lighting designed to be soft yet sufficient. The service is irreproachable, without a hint of servility. All in all dinner at Taillevent is a gala event. The cuisine, incidentally, is in constant progress. Less daring than Senderens' style, it is infinitely more inventive than what you would find at Lasserre—which for a long time many put on an equal footing with Taillevent. The Taillevent style is a "new classicism": witness such dishes as roast prawns with orange butter, red mullet with black olives, fish and seafood pot-au-feu, sweet-and-sour duck garnished with shredded potatoes and mushrooms, veal kidney with preserved shallots, salmis of squab with beef marrow, and the array of delicious desserts.

Each year at vacation time, accompanied by

Taillevent is in a Parisian mansion that once belonged to Napoleon III's half-brother.

his wife, Sabine, Jean-Claude tours the wine regions of France to hunt up new additions to a wine list that is far more than just a sequence of famous names. It is possible to come up with Bordeaux and Burgundies tariffed at around 100 francs that will steady your bill a bit. But if you decide to treat yourself to a really fine old Bordeaux of fifty years or more, you need only ask for it.

A handful of other Parisian restaurant landmarks deserve mention too: Lapérouse is still another example of an endangered monument that was saved in extremis. The food there is not exceptional, but certainly worthy enough to attract diners to its tiny dining rooms and low-ceilinged private salons, where Belle Epoque courtesans used to scratch their names on the mirrors with diamonds, while they supped with their rich protectors.

In the gardens of the Champs-Elysées, across from the presidential palace, two other century-old restaurants have recently been revived: Laurent, redecorated at great cost by British millionaire Jimmy Goldsmith, is one of the best-known rendezvous places for political and business figures. A bit farther down the road is the Pavillon de l'Elysée, taken over and renovated

33

by a real estate promoter who put the celebrated pastry chef Gaston Lenôtre in charge of the kitchens. No visit to Paris would be complete without a luncheon or dinner on the second story of the Eiffel Tower, where not long ago a singularly beautiful luxury restaurant called the Jules Verne opened to great acclaim. It is proving to be an immense success: the food is top-notch and the view of the capital is thrilling.

In this instance, too, huge sums of money were needed to resurrect the historic site. It would seem that large companies are willing to risk investing in such ventures. Maybe someday we shall see the Elysée Palace converted into a restaurant! Stranger things have happened. Long before it became the French White House, the Elysée Palace belonged to Madame de Pompadour. It was confiscated during the French Revolution, and subsequently rented out to an Italian ice cream maker who served meals there!

The taste of well made quenelles is not quickly forgotten. In rouget á l'orientale, Alain Senderens prepares his with eggplant, red snapper, olive oil, and anchovies.

Alain Senderens

ROUGET A L'ORIENTALE

MEDITERRANEAN SNAPPER WITH OLIVE QUENELLES AND A VEGETABLE TART

VEGETABLE TART:

⅓	pound prepared puff pastry
1	baby eggplant, thinly sliced
1	small zucchini, thinly sliced
2	plum tomatoes, thinly sliced
2	tablespoons olive oil
¾	teaspoon thyme

OLIVE QUENELLES:

	Salt
1	small eggplant, halved lengthwise and scored with a sharp knife
2	tablespoons olive oil
1	piece of red snapper fillet (3 ounces), skin removed
15	imported black olives, pitted
2	anchovy fillets

SNAPPER FILLETS AND VEGETABLE GARNISHES:

4	slices ripe tomato, cut about ½-inch thick
	Salt and freshly ground pepper
	About 1 cup olive oil
9	cups parsley leaves
2	tablespoons unsalted butter
6	ripe plum tomatoes, peeled, seeded, and coarsely chopped
	Pinch of saffron threads, diluted in 1 tablespoon hot water
⅓	cup celery leaves
4	red snapper fillets (6 ounces each), skin intact

Prepare vegetable tart: Preheat oven to 400 degrees. On a lightly floured surface, roll out puff pastry to a 10-by-6-inch rectangle; prick all over with a fork. Arrange eggplant, zucchini, and tomato slices on pastry in overlapping lengthwise rows. Brush with olive oil and sprinkle with thyme. Refrigerate for 15 minutes.

Bake tart for about 25 minutes or until vegetables are tender and pastry is golden brown and crisp.

Prepare olive quenelles: Salt cut surfaces of eggplant halves and invert on a rack to drain for 30 minutes. Rinse eggplant and place on a baking sheet. Brush cut sides with 1½ tablespoons olive oil and

bake for about 30 minutes or until tender. Remove eggplant from oven.

In a small skillet, heat remaining olive oil. Add fish fillet and sauté over medium-high heat for about 2 minutes or until it flakes when pierced with a knife. Transfer to a food processor. Scrape eggplant flesh from skins and add to processor with olives and anchovies; purée until blended and set aside.

Prepare snapper fillets and vegetable garnishes: Place tomato slices in a nonmetallic ovenproof dish, season with salt and pepper, and cover with ½ cup olive oil. Bake for 12 minutes or until tender. Transfer tomato slices to paper towels to drain.

Blanch parsley in a large saucepan of boiling salted water for 2 minutes. Drain, wrap in a kitchen towel, and squeeze to extract all moisture. Place parsley in a food processor and purée with butter. Transfer to a small saucepan and season with salt and pepper to taste.

In a small saucepan, combine chopped tomatoes and saffron. Cook over medium-high heat, stirring frequently, for about 10 minutes or until most of the liquid has evaporated and the sauce is chunky. Season with salt and pepper and set aside.

Pour ½ inch olive oil into a small skillet and heat until almost smoking. Add celery leaves and fry for about 10 seconds or until crisped but not brown; drain on paper towels.

In a large skillet, heat 3 tablespoons olive oil. Season snapper fillets with salt and pepper and cut each into thirds on the diagonal. When oil is hot, add fish, skin side down, and sauté over medium-high heat, turning once, for about 9 minutes or until lightly browned and cooked through.

To serve: Reheat quenelle mixture, parsley purée, tomato slices, and tomato sauce. Place a tomato slice topped with parsley purée in center of each of 4 plates. With 2 spoons, shape olive mixture into ovals and place 3 around tomato on each plate. Place a fish fillet at top of quenelles, and top with a little tomato sauce and a few celery leaves. Cut tart into four lengthwise strips and slice each strip into thirds. Place strips between olive quenelles and serve immediately.

Makes 4 servings

Ed. note: The original version of this recipe calls for rouget, *a small Mediterranean fish not found in our* waters.

35

Claude Deligne

SUPREMES DE VOLAILLE
AU FOIE GRAS

CHICKEN BREASTS STUFFED
WITH FOIE GRAS

2	tablespoons unsalted butter
5	pounds chicken backs, chopped
1	large carrot, finely chopped
7	shallots, finely chopped
1	small onion, finely chopped
½	small celery root (celeriac), finely chopped
¼	pound mushrooms, finely chopped
1	clove garlic, finely chopped
½	cup dry vermouth
1	quart rich chicken stock
1	bouquet garni
2	large chicken breasts, halved, boned, and skinned
5	ounces duck foie gras, cut into 8 slices
	Salt and freshly ground pepper
1	egg white
1¼	cups fresh breadcrumbs (from 5 slices white bread, crusts removed)
½	cup crème fraîche
¾	cup unsalted butter, clarified

Preheat oven to 450 degrees.

In a large casserole, melt butter. Add chicken backs and cook over medium heat, stirring for about 10 minutes or until very lightly browned. Add carrot, shallots, onion, celery root, mushrooms, and garlic; stir well, and place in oven. Bake, stirring from time to time, for about 30 minutes or until carcasses and vegetables are nicely browned. Pour contents of casserole into a colander set over a bowl to drain.

Set casserole over medium-high heat and deglaze with vermouth; boil, scraping bottom of casserole with a wooden spoon, for about 3 minutes or until liquid is syrupy. Add stock and bouquet garni and stir well. Return drained carcasses and vegetables to casserole and bring to a boil over high heat. Reduce heat to medium and simmer, skimming as necessary, for 45 minutes.

Meanwhile, remove any large tendons from chicken breasts. Detach fillet from underside of each breast and set aside. With a sharp knife, cut a lengthwise slit in each breast to form a pocket. Place 2 slices of foie gras in each pocket and press to seal shut; replace fillets to completely seal openings.

Bring water to a boil in a steamer. Season breasts with salt and pepper and place them in steamer, smooth side down. Cover and steam for 6 minutes; remove and pat dry. When breasts have cooled slightly, brush them with egg white and roll in breadcrumbs to coat well. Set aside on a rack to dry for about 15 minutes.

Strain rich stock through a fine-mesh strainer set over a saucepan; press hard on bones and vegetables to extract all liquid. Add crème fraîche and bring to a boil over medium-high heat. Simmer sauce, skimming as necessary, for about 15 minutes or until reduced by half. (The sauce should be of a light-coating consistency.)

Just before serving, heat clarified butter in a medium skillet. Add chicken breasts, in batches if necessary, and fry for 2 to 3 minutes per side or until nicely browned. Drain on paper towels. Reheat sauce, if necessary. Spoon some of the sauce onto 4 plates and place a chicken breast half on each. Pass remaining sauce in sauceboat.

Makes 4 servings

Ed. note: The original version of this recipe calls for Bresse chickens. If you can find large, free-range chickens, by all means use them. Remove the breasts for this dish, reserve the legs for another use, and use the carcasses for the sauce.

36

Chicken breasts stuffed with foie gras are served by Claude Deligne at Taillevent with a sauce prepared from, among other things, shallots, celery root, mushrooms, dry vermouth, and rich chicken stock.

MODERN CLASSICS

Chapter

3

ON AN AUTUMN MORNING IN 1976, a secret, closed-door meeting was held in a private room of Michel Guérard's then brand-new, luxurious hotel at Eugénie-les-Bains in the southwestern Landes department of France. The brightest stars of French cuisine were seated at a round table.

The speaker, a man whose features had an air of authority reminiscent of a Roman emperor's, was Paul Bocuse, a name already known throughout the culinary world. He was considered the premier ambassador of French cooking. Along with several colleagues, he had just founded an association for "La Nouvelle Grande Cuisine Française." The aim of the group, holding its first meeting, was to start a promotional campaign for nouvelle cuisine. Bocuse was the undisputed head of the clan, whose members were all old friends. There was Roger Vergé of the Moulin de Mougins, the Troisgros brothers from Roanne, pastry chef Gaston Lenôtre from Paris, Alsatian Paul Haeberlin from Illhaeusern, Alain Chapel from Mionnay, Louis Outhier of La Napoule on the Riviera, René Lasserre, the great Parisian restaurateur, and the "baby" of the group, Michel Guérard. All were famous,

and except for René Lasserre, all were in their prime. These chefs were the vanguard of the new French gastronomy.

Ten years have gone by. The association for "La Nouvelle Grande Cuisine Française" holds no more meetings, for it has since disbanded. The young founders of modern cuisine are now regarded as the forebears of the movement, its founding fathers. Of course, their restaurants still number among the most popular in France, but they are no longer alone in the forefront of innovative cooking; nor have all members of the old association evolved in the same way. Let's pay each of them a visit in their respective restaurants, scattered all over France, to see what they are up to.

A fifteen-minute ride from downtown Lyons, in the Rhône department of France, the restaurant Paul Bocuse is still a mecca for the world's gourmet population. Wedged between the railroad tracks and the Saône River, this large structure of indeterminate style has undergone many changes since the fifties, when young Bocuse, after an apprenticeship with Fernand Point in Vienne and stints at Maxim's and Lucas-Carton, took over for his father. The modest bistro where Bocuse senior served fried fish to the local Sunday fishermen stood, in fact, on the bank of the river a few hundred yards

The real Paul Bocuse is standing here in front of a photorealist painting by the artist Olivier Hucleux and beside a bronze sculpture by Daniel Druet. Bocuse is France's premier ambassador of nouvelle cuisine.

away from the restaurant's current site.

Bocuse still speaks nostalgically of the family inn, handed down from father to son since the eighteenth century. More rarely does he sigh, as he used to do, "What really would have made me happy would have been to stay right there and cook for twenty people at a time." Relatively speaking, Bocuse has become a multinational enterprise, and it is highly unlikely that he will ever look back. Indeed, his success has compelled him to enlarge his restaurant, making it a little more grandiose every year. More partial to spectacular effects than to refined intimacy, he has "staged" his restaurant as others might stage an opera.

At the foot of the restaurant's steps, a young black man wearing a red uniform opens car doors for customers and escorts them through the small garden up to the large glass entrance. Beyond, behind a bay window, can be seen the huge, splendid kitchens where a score of employees bustle about. Until recently, guests were always greeted at the dining room door by the smiling, gracious Raymonde, Madame Bocuse. But these days, she is on hand only occasionally. Instead, there is Joël Fleury, formerly chef of the Frantel hotel in Lyons, who traded in his white chef's jacket for the dark suit of a dining room manager. It is whispered that Bocuse may one day turn the restaurant over to Fleury, but no official announcement has borne out the rumor. Joël Fleury will leave you in the care of the head waiter in charge of your table. There is a large dining room on the upper floor, generally occupied by groups; most guests are given a table on the ground floor, either in the principal dining room or in the rotunda whose window-wall affords a view of trees and the swiftly flowing Saône.

The recently renovated decor is an indescrib-able mix of styles and colors. The whole is perfectly comfortable, however, and the well spaced tables are elegantly laid. Bocuse's presence is pervasive: the famous face peers out at diners from pictures and posters, from the menu, even from the cardboard napkin rings. Some wags comment that Bocuse is on the walls more than he is in the kitchen, but they exaggerate. Even when he is away, he knows how to make his presence felt. Bocuse can also be seen on television and in the press, making pitches for stoves, Beaujolais, food products, and airlines. Piles of his many cookbooks are prominently on display. He even has a restaurant in Epcot, Florida, which he started with pals Vergé and Lenôtre. When he is at his restaurant, however, he welcomes unknown faces as warmly as old friends.

Bocuse is not one of those innovative cooks who never cease perfecting their new creations or inventing new flavor combinations. In fact, like most Lyonnais he has always been a traditionalist. In the nouvelle cuisine movement, he was a leader, a figurehead more than an inventive cook. It was he who first dared to give top billing to simple dishes that he prepared better than anyone else: crunchy green beans, very slightly cooked rock fish, a spit-roasted Bresse chicken, or the world's best potato and leek soup. He had the nerve and the genius to rid "grande cuisine" of needless fussiness and heavy sauces and to serve dishes that did not alter the natural taste of food.

It was in this regard that he was an innovator, but he has left behind no lasting creations comparable to those of Guérard, or Senderens, Jacques Maximin, Alain Chapel, and others. His two signature dishes are the truffle soup "Valéry Giscard d'Estaing" and bass in pastry. The first is derived from an old specialty of Haeberlin, and the second was a recipe of his mentor, Fernand Point. It would be wrong, then, to visit Bocuse in hopes of finding imaginative, resolutely modern cuisine. Roger Jaloux, his chef, occasionally includes on the menu dishes that fall into the "modern" category, like turbot with truffle- and chive-flavored lobster ravioli or sweetbreads with coriander and girolle mushrooms, but they are not the restaurant's best offerings. Rather, he excels in preparations that may seem self-evident and countrified, like the famous green bean salad or the chicken with peas, or others, such as the frog and crayfish soup with watercress; green asparagus served with an amazing vinaigrette made with Beaujolais and mustard; a marvelous pot-au-feu of duck with coarse salt accompanied by another great vinaigrette made with hazelnut oil; duck with turnips and green olives; divine vanilla ice cream; and a no less admirable bitter chocolate ice.

In fact, Bocuse is the best place in all of France to eat bourgeois cooking. Don't feel obliged to order costly wines. The restaurant has no wine steward—Bocuse is opposed to them—and the head waiter encourages you to drink the Beaujolais selected especially for Bocuse by Georges Duboeuf. They are excellent in fact and allow you to spend less at Bocuse's place than in most of the great restaurants of France. Before leaving, request a tour of the annex: an immense room that holds a fabulous mechanical organ worked by the mechanical figures that Bocuse collects. The sight of Bocuse himself starting up the machine is unforgettable; circus and show-biz are what he loves above all else.

It might never cross a traveler's mind to visit Roanne, an unremarkable town one hour's drive from Lyons, whose reputation, such as it was,

came from the arms factory and textile industry located there. Back in the 1960s, two brothers, Pierre and Jean Troisgros, ran a family restaurant at the Hôtel Moderne. Outside, it resembled any other little provincial hotel of the type that abounds in France, but what a difference inside! You would never have guessed that you were in a restaurant, for it seemed much more like a home, and you were immediately adopted as a member of the family.

First, there was the man that the entire staff called "Boss": Jean-Baptiste Troisgros, son of a Burgundy winegrowing family that had opened this modest establishment in Roanne. Gifted with an extraordinary temperament, this man who had received no education whatsoever was a veritable poet. He invented words of his own and spoke enthrallingly about life, women, and, above all, about wine. He undoubtedly had one of the most delicate palates I've ever encountered. He had definite ideas, some even a bit eccentric; it was he, for example, who launched the fashion of chilling certain red wines. Jean-Baptiste was not a chef himself, much to his

41

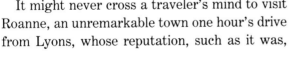
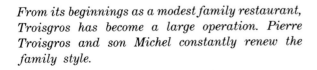

From its beginnings as a modest family restaurant, Troisgros has become a large operation. Pierre Troisgros and son Michel constantly renew the family style.

regret. To compensate, he was determined to turn his sons, Jean and Pierre, into the world's best cooks. Every day at noon, he settled down in the dining room, where their latest creations were set before him. If he didn't like something, Jean-Baptiste flew into a mock fury; since he was always right, Pierre and Jean accepted his judgment. Either they altered the dish, or they removed it from the menu.

And then there was *maman*, a Burgundian matron of few words. Whenever her husband brought a great Burgundy up from the wine cellar, she would taste it and, if it pleased her, comment: "You see, Jean-Baptiste, this wine of yours doesn't bother me at all." Coming from her, it was a tremendous compliment. At the cash register was *Tata*, Madame Troisgros' sister, an unobtrusive lady in black. She too said very little, but she helped keep the house running smoothly. The two daughters-in-law were on hand as well: Jean's wife, Maria, a tall, handsome woman, and lively Olympe, a brunette of Italian extraction, married to Pierre. The two brothers, working in their tiny, cramped kitchen, were a study in opposites: Jean, slim and rather reserved, and Pierre, chubby and jovial.

Though it may not have looked like anything extraordinary was happening, the pair were in fact inventing what would soon be known as the "Troisgros style": a free, spontaneous cuisine that was diametrically opposed to the pretentious, grandiloquent style prepared at Maxim's, Lucas-Carton, and other luxury establishments. They drew new inspiration daily from the market's seasonal bounty and the riches of the region. They gave a different, special savor to everything they cooked. They could turn a simple roast chicken into something sublime; frogs fished from local ponds at night by passing Gypsies were a revelation. In those days, their most successful specialties were thrush pâté, fresh salmon with sorrel, and Charolais beef with marrow in Fleurie wine. But every meal afforded new pleasures and discoveries.

The brothers made such a name for themselves that soon journalists were flocking in from all over, crowds were clamoring for tables, and, for the first time in memory, tourists invaded Roanne. Over the years, the Troisgros family renovated, embellished, and enlarged their inn; with time, Troisgros became a veritable institution, where would-be cooks lined up outside the door for training sessions.

Time darkened this bright picture. Jean-Baptiste, followed by Madame Troisgros, her sister, Maria, and then, finally, Jean, all passed away. Their deaths left an enormous void that Pierre and Olympe, the survivors, tried their best to fill, helped by their son Michel, who now assists his father in the kitchen. Troisgros today is obviously much different from Troisgros in happier days. You can no longer hoist a glass of Gevrey-Chambertin at the bar, the inn's little rooms have given way to suites, a squad of waiters serves one hundred meals a day, and in the kitchens—the largest, best equipped in France—a brigade of over twenty men and women are busy at the stoves.

The dishes that brought the restaurant to fame are still on the menu, but in the course of their extensive travels, Pierre and Jean enthusiastically adopted techniques and flavors culled from foreign—especially Asiatic—cuisines. The Troisgros style was brought up to date, with dishes that would probably have astounded old Jean-Baptiste: hot oysters with black radish, caramelized foie gras with rhubarb, or Chinese-style banana fritters.

Some of these recent creations are highly successful, others less so. Pierre and Michel Troisgros seem to draw their best inspiration from traditional, regional sources. The inimitable grace of their cuisine comes from that brilliant mix of rusticity, simplicity, and refinement that brought a breath of fresh air into the pompous precincts of grande cuisine. When dining at Troisgros, order such dishes as the frogs and snails with a vegetable ratatouille; the chicken wings with mushrooms, horseradish, and truffles; the salmon served in its crusty, totally degreased skin; the little chunks of sweetbreads with shallots and spinach; the calf's head ragoût with olives; chicken with aged wine vinegar; and any of the scrumptious desserts, from the very classic snow eggs to the extraordinary lime and jasmine flan. Don't pass by the splendiferous Burgundies or Beaujolais or the aged Cognacs from the sumptuous Troisgros collection.

People say the Haeberlin brothers just as they always say the Troisgros brothers, but only one of the Haeberlin brothers is a chef: that being Paul, a corpulent, portly Alsatian, whose stature and epicurean grin give him the air of an old-fashioned chef whose sole interest lies in the kitchen. Small, slim, and loquacious, brother Jean-Pierre is just the opposite. He studied at the Beaux-Arts school of Strasbourg; he is a gifted draftsman. Jean-Pierre executes oils and watercolors, one of which adorns the menu. Ardently interested in antiques, he has filled the old family inn at Illhaeusern, a little village near Colmar, with fine old furniture and Alsatian faience stoves. He has also rebuilt the delightful three-hundred-year-old wooden house in the garden, where groups are sometimes served before the fireplace.

The Auberge de l'Ill, as the inn is called, possesses a special charm. It sits on the bank of a romantic river where the flat-bottomed boats of the last river fishermen (hoping to net river perch or pike) still glide in the shade of the willows. The entire family welcomes guests warmly into this house, which over the years has grown in size and beauty. A table must be reserved far in advance, for the German border is just a stone's throw away, and, on weekends, German visitors are drawn by the inn's reputation and a favorable rate of exchange.

Though he was trained classically, Paul Haeberlin has been influenced by nouvelle cuisine. He is not an orthodox practitioner of the modern art, but he regularly lightens his dishes and occasionally gives them a contemporary air. The arrival of his son Marc on the kitchen front accelerated the movement, though not always successfully. Alsace is a very conservative place, for one thing, and, for another, neither Marc nor his father is totally at ease with nouvelle cuisine. Lately, they have been digging more and more into the regional repertory of Alsace, adding their own personal touch and producing results that would be hard to improve.

Sample the partridge broth with girolle mushrooms, foie gras, and cabbage, brought to the table boiling hot beneath a crust of golden puff pastry; the warm salad of green lentils with hog's jowls and goose liver; carp cooked in Alsatian Pinot Noir; a stuffed pig's trotter braised in Alsatian Tokay; the exquisite pot-au-feu of beef filet and goose liver, seasoned with coarse salt and aromatic herbs; or in game season (September–October) a young wild partridge garnished with green wheat.

A visit chez Haeberlin is also the perfect occasion to get to know the great white wines of Alsace. They are, chauvinism aside, far superior to their German cousins. The wine list at the Auberge de l'Ill is nothing short of fabulous, and with a "late harvest" Riesling from Hugel or a venerable Tokay from Trimbach or Schlumberger, one will spend a memorable few hours.

With Alain Chapel, we truly enter the world of creative cuisine. Although he never wished to be linked with a particular school, this son of an ultraconservative innkeeping family from the countryside near Lyons unquestionably brought a new, personal tone to French cuisine. His chef friends and colleagues consider Chapel to be the most knowledgeable of them all. He transformed his unprepossessing little family inn, which stands by the roadside in the village of Mionnay, into an elegant establishment. With its indoor garden enclosed by an arcaded gallery, the place has a Provençal air about it that is unexpected in this land of ponds and swamps, peopled by myriad birds. In summer guests are seated in the cool of the gallery, in winter in the charming dining room with its pink stone floor and white stone fireplace. Flowers abound; the room is a jewel of elegant simplicity.

Alain Chapel is reserved, less a restaurateur than a chef; he does not glad-hand his guests, and his otherwise charming house lacks the harmony and feeling of comfort that one normally expects to find. The welcome is tepid, the service kind but not always very precise, and some have complained that the cooking is inconsistent. Could this complaint be due to the atmosphere?—guests are often as sensitive to the reception as they are to the cooking.

Guests are usually started off with an aperitif—pink Champagne, for example—in the garden or the little salon next to the dining room while they wait. There will probably be some delightful pre-dinner nibbles—tiny fried fish and fried parsley, a thyme- and pepper-scented aspic of young rabbit, or tuna with ginger. The menu and the fixed-price meals change so often it's impossible to have favorites, but let me describe my last meal at Alain Chapel's. There was a cream of clams and sea urchins; small red mullet served with coriander stems and tops heightened by a sauce with just a hint of mustard; a ragoût of Breton lobster garnished with marvelous miniature red potatoes that were at once firm and tender; a casserole of small wild birds served with a risotto braised in the cooking juices; admirable goat cheeses, one fresh, one

ripened; and, finally, a fantastic bitter chocolate marquise. Chapel got the recipe from an old farmwoman, and he guards it as jealously as a family secret. The vanilla and cinnamon ice cream is like nothing to be found in a soda shop! The wine cellar is one of the richest in France, with a staggering (and costly) collection of Chambertins, Richebourgs, Hermitages, and Bordeaux as well, for, even at the Burgundian border, people drink as much Bordeaux as Burgundy. For all this, Chapel does not sell himself cheap; indeed, his is one of the most expensive restaurants in France.

Alain Chapel's place may give you the feeling of being in Provence, but, at Roger Vergé's place, not far from Cannes, you know you're really there. Nowadays all the celebrities who visit the Riviera stop off at this pretty, sun-drenched house, Le Moulin de Mougins, where the big mill wheel is still to be seen, just beside a delightful, closed garden surrounded by thick walls of greenery. "Except for the Pope," says Vergé, "I can't think of a single great name that hasn't passed through here." On summer evenings, he serves 150 meals (reserve a garden table), 90 percent of them to foreigners, among them Arab princes and Texas billionaires.

To describe the kind of cooking he does, Vergé uses the expressive phrase, "It's the cuisine of the sun." Its clarity, its free use of aromatic herbs and local vegetables, its light sauces and keen flavors, make it a typically Provençal cuisine with which Vergé mixes his own ideas, know-how, and very personal style. While he isn't a southerner himself (he comes from the center of France) he has totally absorbed the spirit of Provence. Vergé is a true creator. Although the cooking of, say, Bocuse has had no influence on the younger generation of cooks, Vergé's "cuisine of the sun" has left its mark on many an up-and-coming chef.

Each year, about fifty new dishes are added to the list of favorite specialties like the violet artichokes à la barigoule (sautéed in olive oil and white wine); the gâteau of rabbit in Chablis; spiny lobster with pink peppercorns; lobster in Sauternes; filet of bass with shallots and white Provençal wine; noisettes of lamb with truffle purée; or pigeon with garlic and endives. Among recent and exciting discoveries at the Moulin are the sautéed Provençal vegetables with a wild mushroom purée; truffle-stuffed zucchini blossoms; sage leaf fritters (the batter is so light it seems transparent); tiny red mullet with tomatoes and herb-scented olive oil; baked turbot sprinkled with chervil-flavored oil; and the tender, pink filet of veal with tomato purée. The entire array of desserts, which used to be a bit pale, is now superb.

Everyone wants to be on hand for dinner, so the waiting list is miles long during the height of the summer season. Yet at lunchtime there is plenty of room and a good time to reserve for those not afraid of feeling a little alone. The staff has more time, the kitchen is less rushed, their work is more consistent. At whatever time, it's going to cost. The wines are excellent and expensive. The Burgundies, however, command lower prices than do the Bordeaux; and for those who like a Provençal wine, the Château Vignelaure, the Château Simone, and the Château Pradeaux, a delicious red Bandol, are the best in the house.

Louis Outhier has transformed a tumble-down house in La Napoule, a little pleasure port near Cannes, into an opulent, even slightly ostentatious, restaurant, L'Oasis. The Louis XV decor seems somehow out of place in the light and atmosphere of the Riviera; try to reserve one of the few tables in the glassed-in gallery

45

The dessert tray is an eye-catcher at Alain Chapel's restaurant, Au Trou Gascon. Chapel jealously guards the secret of his bitter chocolate marquise.

that borders the lovely indoor garden.

Along with Bocuse and the Troisgros brothers, Louis Outhier was one of Fernand Point's last pupils. A shy, nervous man, he was greatly influenced by Point early in his career, but his own style developed progressively. Back in the 1960s his specialties were bass in pastry (like Bocuse), truffle in puff pastry, and whole veal kidney in sherry. Outhier seemed to be getting into a rut until, a few years ago, his style underwent a dramatic change when he traveled to the Far East. The Hotel Oriental in Bangkok had invited him to supervise the cuisine prepared in their French restaurant, and there Outhier became fascinated with exotic spices and herbs. In a surprising turnabout, this ultraconservative cook was transformed into an enthusiastic creator.

Classics like his egg with caviar, his turbot braised in Champagne, hen with morels, John Dory in red wine, or strips of duck breast in Armagnac—excellent dishes, incidentally—are still on his menu. He is a master craftsman of this traditional sort of repertory, but it is in the other, more creative register that Outhier is a veritable artist. Ask for his prawn soup with Japanese tapioca, lemon thyme, and hot pepper; or the skate with truffles, lemon, and white wine vinegar; or perhaps his marvelous spiny lobster with Thai herbs (lemongrass, ginger, curry, and apples); the sliced lamb with ginger and fava beans; or the crusty duck Oriental, served with a sensational sauce that features honey, coriander, and Thai herbs. Outhier's cuisine may leave some palates bemused, but, to my mind, it is an experience not to be missed. Don't forget to save room for dessert. Gilles Falaschi, the Oasis pastry chef, is an artist in his own right, and it is nigh impossible to keep a cool head when confronted by his spectacular dessert trolley.

We began our visit to the founding fathers of nouvelle cuisine at Michel Guérard's beautiful house in the Landes, and we will end it there, for it has become an international symbol of French elegance and taste. This youthful man of fifty with the face of a choir boy is undoubtedly the most energetic, enthusiastic, and innovative member of the old association. The son of a butcher, Guérard has worked in kitchens since the age of seventeen. He soon rebelled against the humdrum routine that tied chefs down in those days. Like Vergé, he met Bocuse and the Troisgros brothers in 1962; the need for freedom that had long been gnawing him finally became irresistible. After the encounter he wrote in his diary: "From now on I'm going to cook the way the bird sings!" He started out in a dingy Parisian suburb where he ran a little bistro called the Pot-au-Feu. Despite the locale, it was clear that a great cook had just emerged on the scene.

Guérard had swift and phenomenal success with chic Parisians, who found it amusing to ride out to the capital's industrial boondocks for a meal. But soon afterward, our young chef married; his wife, Christine, carried him off to the southwest of France, to Eugénie-les-Bains, a small, Napoleon III-era thermal spa, which the bride's father was attempting to revive. It seemed a risky venture, and Guérard's friends tried to dissuade him. Who would pay attention to fine cuisine in an out-of-the-way spot like that?

As it happened, Guérard's hunch was correct. When he opened in the month of March, he found he had a full house, with guests from all over the world. Miraculously, nothing could be less "touristy" than this spacious white house surrounded by woods and fields. The wrought-iron balconies that bring New Orleans to mind,

In summer the waiting list is miles long for Roger Vergé's Provençal cuisine at Le Moulin de Mougins on the Riviera.

the palm and banana trees that flourish in the mild climate of France's southwest, the Romantic paintings, the mahogany furniture, the Art Nouveau curios, the tables all festively laid, the bottles of aged Armagnac and pots of jam neatly aligned on shelves—every single detail is ravishing. A feeling of serenity and intimacy reigns at Michel Guérard, unexpected in a house where so many people come and go.

Those fortunate enough to visit the kitchens with Guérard will grasp the special spirit of the place. The team of fifteen men and women directed by chef Didier Oudil seem more like a group of friends than a typical kitchen brigade. A mood of cooperation reigns as they inspect the baskets of wild mushrooms gathered that morning, the foies gras fresh from their wrappers, the just-picked herbs still wet with dew. The illusion of improvisation ends when Guérard gets to work. Despite his occasionally disheveled appearance, he is a born organizer. He puts each dish together with the precision of a chemist, particularly when it's one of his "light cuisine" specialties. Guérard's low-calorie cooking is the best of its type on earth. It allows those taking the slimming cure to shed several pounds in ten days while they indulge in crayfish, lobster, pigeon, and even rich-looking desserts. Low-calorie cuisine demands particularly painstaking attention from the chef, but Guérard's results are frankly amazing. Anyone spending a couple of days at Michel and Christine's inn should have at least one "light" meal (one thousand calories). Your tastebuds won't believe that it is diet food.

The majority of guests don't return to Eugénie-les-Bains to lose weight, but rather to enjoy what Guérard so prettily terms his "cuisine gourmande," food lover's food: it is ever-changing, as beautiful to behold as it is heavenly to eat. Every one of his creations is captivating, whether it is the fresh foie gras with pepper; the little truffle- or morel-stuffed ravioli; the whole roasted lobster smoked right in the fireplace; the salmon served with lemon-flavored crayfish fritters; skate roasted in bacon slices with a sauce that includes Graves wine and lobster coral; the daube of local duck and pig's trotters, the squab with cabbage; the farm-raised chicken with parsley; or any of the divine desserts: from the thin, hot apple tart (often imitated, never equaled) to the cornucopia of glacéed fruit.

Michel Guérard's brand of cooking is the epitome of anti-"grande cuisine." There is a pinch of genius in these dishes, too, in the transformation of simple, direct, rustic flavors by a seemingly inexhaustible imagination. But watch out: Eugénie-les-Bains casts a bewitching spell; people have been known to go one day for lunch and, two days later, find themselves still there.

Cerfeuil

Michel Guérard's cuisine owes its flavor to the fresh herbs he harvests daily. Facing page: Christine and Michel Guérard.

Paul Bocuse

SAUMON OU LOUP EN CROUTE
FERNAND POINT, SAUCE CHORON

SALMON OR STRIPED BASS
IN PASTRY WITH
CHORON SAUCE

SALMON:
1	tablespoon olive oil
2½	to 3 pounds salmon or striped bass fillets from whole fish, skin removed and central bone detached, but reserved, optional
1	tablespoon finely chopped parsley
1	tablespoon finely chopped chervil
2	teaspoons finely chopped tarragon
	Salt and freshly ground pepper to taste
½	to ¾ pounds puff pastry, fresh or frozen
1	tablespoon unsalted butter
1	egg yolk

SIMPLIFIED CHORON SAUCE:
¼	cup wine vinegar
2	tablespoons finely chopped shallots
2	tablespoons finely chopped tarragon
	Salt and freshly ground pepper to taste
2	egg yolks
2	tablespoons water
½	cup plus 2 tablespoons cold butter, cut into pieces
	Juice of 1 lemon
1	teaspoon tomato paste
1	tablespoon finely chopped chervil

Prepare fish: Brush a large plate with oil and place fish on it. Sprinkle herbs on both sides of each fillet; season with salt and pepper to taste.

Butter a baking dish large enough to hold fish and line with a piece of buttered parchment paper of the same size.

On a floured board, evenly roll pastry into 2 rectangles the size of the fish. Place one rectangle in the prepared pan and lay fish on top of it. With a brush dipped in water, moisten edges of pastry. Place second layer of pastry on top of fish. Cut pastry around fillets to form a fish shape, making a head, tail, and fins. Lightly press edges of pastry to seal. With the wide end of a small metal pastry tube tip, make impressions on pastry to resemble fish scales. Use scraps to decorate fish with an eye, gills, and fins. Brush yolk over fish to glaze.

Bake fish in preheated oven for about 15 minutes, reduce temperature to 350 degrees, and continue to bake for another 20 to 30 minutes (cooking time will depend on thickness of fish).

Prepare sauce: In a small, heavy enamel or tin-lined saucepan, combine vinegar, shallots, 1 tablespoon tarragon, and salt and pepper to taste. Bring to a boil over medium heat and reduce until shallots and tarragon are wet, but liquid has evaporated. Remove from heat and cool. Add egg yolks and water to saucepan or transfer to double boiler and cook, whisking constantly, over very low heat. (Have heated sauceboat on hand, as sauce will not keep.) Whisk in butter, lemon juice, and tomato paste and continue whisking for about 5 minutes or until sauce is light and thickened. Season to taste and add chervil and remaining tarragon. Keep sauce warm.

To serve: When fish is cooked, lift pastry crust at one end with a sharp knife; lift top fillet with a spatula and remove central bone. Place fish on serving platter, replace top crust, and serve with choron sauce.

Makes 6 servings

50

Paul Bocuse first wraps salmon or striped bass in a pastry crust, bakes it, and serves it with sauce choron.

Paul Bocuse

VOLAILLE DE BRESSE HALLOWEEN

CHICKEN AND RICE COOKED IN A PUMPKIN WITH A PUMPKIN GRATIN

8-	to 9-pound round pumpkin, washed and dried
4½	pound free-range chicken, at room temperature
	Salt and freshly ground pepper
1	bunch fresh tarragon
10	sprigs parsley
6	tablespoons unsalted butter
1	cup rice
2	cups water
2	eggs, beaten with 1 cup heavy cream
	Freshly grated nutmeg
2	ounces Gruyère cheese, grated

Preheat oven to 400 degres.

Cut a hat, about 4 inches from top of pumpkin; remove and set aside. With a large, sturdy spoon, scoop out pumpkin seeds and discard. Scoop out pumpkin flesh, leaving a ½-inch shell; reserve flesh. Cover pumpkin shell with aluminum foil and place on a baking sheet.

Season cavity of chicken with salt and pepper and stuff with tarragon, parsley, and 4 tablespoons but-ter. Truss chicken and place it in pumpkin, breast side up. Replace hat on pumpkin, cover with alumi-num foil, and bake for 2 hours. Soak rice in water.

Meanwhile, cook reserved pumpkin flesh in boiling salted water for 10 minutes. Drain well and transfer to an ovenproof casserole. Bake in preheated oven, stirring from time to time, for about 40 minutes or until pumpkin is quite dry. (This can also be done on the stove.)

Whisk egg-cream mixture into pumpkin. (For a smoother mixture, purée pumpkin in a food processor with egg-cream mixture.) Season with salt and pep-per to taste. Butter a medium gratin dish with remaining butter, add pumpkin mixture, and sprinkle with nutmeg and grated cheese.

Remove chicken from pumpkin. Drain rice and add to pumpkin, then replace chicken and the "hat." Bake chicken for about 1 hour or until the juices run clear when the thigh is pierced with a skewer and the rice is tender.

About 20 minutes before chicken is done, place pumpkin gratin in oven and bake until cheese is melted and mixture is heated through.

To serve: Remove chicken from pumpkin and dis-card trussing strings. Carve chicken into serving pieces. With a large spoon, scoop rice into a serving bowl. Serve chicken immediately, accompanied by rice and pumpkin gratin.

Makes 6 to 8 servings

51

Volaille de Bresse Halloween was made with American traditions in mind.

Pierre and Michel Troisgros
BRILLANT AU CARAMEL
CHOCOLATE CARAMEL TART

7	ounces sweet pie pastry
1⅓	cups heavy cream
3½	ounces semisweet chocolate, melted
¾	cup sugar
1	tablespoon plus 1 teaspoon light corn syrup
3	tablespoons water
1½	teaspoons fresh lemon juice

Preheat oven to 350 degrees. On a lightly floured surface, roll out pastry to a 9-inch circle. Place on a heavy baking sheet and bake for about 14 minutes or until golden brown. Transfer to a rack to cool.

In a small saucepan, scald ⅓ cup cream over medium-high heat. Remove from heat and stir in melted chocolate. Set aside to cool, stirring occasionally, until mixture is just firm enough to hold its shape.

Spread a thin layer of chocolate mixture over pastry circle. Scrape remaining chocolate mixture into a pastry bag fitted with a medium star tip. Pipe chocolate around rim of pastry to form a border; then, starting at center of pastry, pipe the outline of 8 pie wedges. Refrigerate for about 30 minutes or until firm.

Meanwhile, make the caramel. In a heavy saucepan, combine sugar, corn syrup, and water. Bring to a boil over medium heat and cook for about 12 minutes or until lightly golden. Remove from heat and stir in remaining cream. (The mixture may sputter, so watch carefully.) Bring caramel to a boil over medium-high heat, stirring constantly. Remove from heat and stir in lemon juice. Let caramel cool to room temperature.

When caramel is cool, spoon it into the 8 outlined pie sections. Refrigerate tart for 30 minutes before serving, if desired.

Makes 8 servings

Brillant au Caramel, at the left, is one of Pierre and Michel Troisgros' tempting desserts.

Paul, Jean-Pierre,
and Marc Haeberlin

MOUSSELINE DE GRENOUILLES
FROG MOUSSELINES WITH SPINACH

½   cup plus 2 tablespoons unsalted butter
4   shallots, finely chopped
4½   pounds fresh frogs' legs
1⅔   cups Alsatian Riesling
     Salt and freshly ground pepper
½   pound pike or perch fillets
2   egg whites
3   cups heavy cream, well chilled
1   pound fresh spinach leaves, washed and large
     stems removed
1   clove garlic, unpeeled
½   tablespoon unsalted butter blended with ½
     tablespoon flour
     Fresh lemon juice
     Snipped fresh chives

Place bowl and steel blade of a food processor in freezer.

In a large sauté pan, melt 1½ tablespoons butter. Add shallots and sauté over medium-high heat, stirring constantly, for about 3 minutes or until translucent. Add half the frogs' legs, wine, and a pinch of salt and pepper. Bring to a simmer, stir well, and cover; cook, stirring from time to time, for 10 minutes.

Remove frogs' legs from skillet and set aside. Strain cooking liquid through a fine-mesh strainer set over a medium saucepan. Bring liquid to a boil and cook over medium-high heat, skimming as necessary, for about 9 minutes or until reduced by half.

Bone remaining raw frogs' legs. Remove bowl and blade from freezer, add fish fillets and frog meat, and purée. With machine running, gradually add egg whites; when whites are fully incorporated, gradually add 2 cups cream. Scrape mousseline into a medium bowl and blend in ¾ teaspoon salt and 8 grindings of fresh pepper. Refrigerate.

Bone cooked frogs' legs. Preheat oven to 325 degrees.

(Recipe continued on following page.)

53

Mousseline de grenouilles is a delicate specialty of Les Haeberlins.

Butter ten ⅔-cup ramekins. Scrape mousseline into a pastry bag fitted with a round tip. Pipe mixture into ramekins to generously cover bottoms and sides, and fill centers with some of the cooked frog meat. Cover and fill in with remaining mousseline; smooth surfaces with a flat spatula. Place filled ramekins in a hot water bath, cover with parchment paper, and bake for 15 to 19 minutes or until firm.

Meanwhile, blanch spinach leaves in boiling, salted water for 1 minute; drain well. In a medium skillet, melt 2 tablespoons butter with the garlic. When butter foams, add spinach and cook over medium heat, tossing gently, for about 2 minutes or until heated through. Cover and keep warm.

Bring reduced cooking liquid to a boil over medium-high heat. Whisk in butter-flour mixture, a little at a time, and bring to a boil. Add remaining 1 cup cream and return to a boil, whisking constantly. Remove from heat and whisk in remaining 6½ tablespoons butter, one tablespoon at a time. Season to taste with salt, pepper, and lemon juice. Add remaining cooked frog meat to sauce and rewarm.

Spoon some sauce onto each plate and arrange spinach in center. Unmold mousselines, draining if necessary, and place over spinach. Top with remaining sauce and sprinkle each serving with chives.

Makes 10 servings

Pierre and Michel Troisgros

MIXED BOEUF

FIVE CUTS OF BEEF WITH RED WINE AND SHALLOTS

1	cut dry red wine
3	shallots, thickly sliced
	Pinch of sugar
	Salt and freshly ground pepper
5	tablespoons unsalted butter
8½	ounces heart of tenderloin, cut 1¼-inches thick
½	pound boneless rib steak, cut ½-inch thick
6	ounces sirloin tip, cut into 4 slices
7	ounces boneless top loin, cut into 4 slices
6	ounces flank steak, cut into 4 slices

The Troisgros dish of five cuts of beef can be prepared easily and quickly.

In a small, noncorrodible saucepan, combine wine and shallots with a pinch each of sugar and salt; bring to a boil and set aside.

Season meats with salt and pepper. In both a small and a medium skillet, melt 1½ tablespoons butter over medium-high heat. When butter begins to foam, add tenderloin to the small skillet and rib steak to the medium skillet. Cook tenderloin for 8 minutes, turning once; cook rib steak for 5 minutes, turning once. Remove meats from skillets and set meats and skillets aside.

In a large skillet, heat remaining 2 tablespoons butter until foaming. Add sirloin, top loin, and flank steak slices, in batches if necessary, and cook over medium-high heat, turning once, for 2 to 4 minutes (depending on thickness of meat). Remove meat from skillet and divide evenly among 4 heated plates.

Cut both tenderloin and rib steak into 4 slices and place on plates.

Discard fat from all 3 skillets and set them over high heat. Deglaze skillets with shallot-wine mixture; season with salt and pepper to taste and pour this sauce over meats. Serve immediately.

Makes 4 servings
Ed. note: The French like their meat rare; if you prefer yours better done, add a few minutes to the cooking times given here.

Paul, Jean-Pierre, and Marc Haeberlin

LE TURBOTIN ROTI A L'AIL ET AUX LARDONS

CHICKEN TURBOT ROASTED WITH GARLIC AND BACON

2   whole chicken turbots, 2½ pounds each, cleaned and skinned, or substitute grey sole or flounder

½   cup flour seasoned with salt and pepper to taste

1   tablespoon olive oil

½   pound slab bacon, cut into ⅓-by-1½-inch strips

12   cloves garlic, unpeeled

2   tablespoons finely chopped shallots

3   tablespoons aged sherry wine vinegar

½   cup veal or chicken stock

½   cup crème fraîche

½   cup cold unsalted butter, cut into small pieces

Leaf spinach or green cabbage leaves, blanched and lightly sautéed in butter, for serving

Preheat oven to 400 degrees.

Lightly coat fish with seasoned flour; brush off any excess. In an ovenproof skillet large enough to hold both fish, heat oil. Add fish and sauté over medium heat until golden on one side. Turn fish and add bacon and garlic. When the second side is golden, place skillet in preheated oven and bake for 8 to 10 minutes or until garlic is soft inside and fish is just cooked. Transfer fish to a heated serving dish and spoon garlic and bacon on top; cover with aluminum foil and keep warm.

Pour off excess fat from skillet and add shallots. Sauté over medium heat until softened. Deglaze with vinegar. Add stock and crème fraîche and stir with a wooden spoon. Reduce over medium heat for about 2 minutes or until thickened. Whisk in butter, a few pieces at a time, and cook over low heat until creamy.

To serve, pour sauce over warm fish and accompany with spinach or green cabbage.

Makes 4 servings

55

Overleaf: Flounder and chicken are equally suitable as the focus of this dish, which includes baked garlic and bacon.

Alain Chapel

DES COQUILLAGES A LA FACON D'ESCARGOTS

MOLLUSKS (OR SHELLFISH) IN THE STYLE OF SNAILS

1¾	pound winkles, washed
½	pound tiny littleneck clams, washed
½	pound tiny cockles, washed and scrubbed
¼	pound tiny crabs, if available
2	cups court bouillon
½	pound mixed soup herbs: garden cress, celery leaves, parsley, chervil, nettles, leek greens, chives, and purslane
1	cup unsalted butter, softened, plus 1 tablespoon butter
	Salt and freshly ground pepper
¼	teaspoon minced garlic
¼	teaspoon anchovy paste
	Juice of ½ lemon
¼	teaspoon anise
16	central stalks from Romaine or Boston lettuce or substitute 4 stalks celery, cut into strips
1	spring onion, finely chopped
1	shallot, finely chopped
2	firm, ripe medium tomatoes, peeled, seeded, and finely chopped
24	large sea snail shells

58

Preheat oven to 450 degrees. In a saucepan, combine winkles, clams, cockles, tiny crabs, and court bouillon. Cover and cook over high heat for 3 to 5 minutes; cool and strain, reserving court bouillon. Extract fish from shells; use a needle to remove winkles and a small knife for cockles and clams. Leave tiny crabs whole. Reserve all fish in a bowl with some court bouillon.

Blanch soup herbs in 3 to 4 quarts boiling, salted water for about 3 minutes; transfer to a bowl of ice water to cool. Drain and chop finely. Mix herbs with softened butter and season to taste with salt, pepper, garlic, anchovy paste, lemon juice, and anise; reserve.

In a saucepan, cover lettuce with boiling, salted water and cook until softened. Remove from heat and reserve in about 2 tablespoons cooking liquid. In a heavy saucepan, melt 1 tablespoon butter. Add onion and shallot and cook over low heat. Add lettuce stems and tomatoes. Cook, stirring with a wooden spoon, and moisten with reserved cooking liquid; simmer and reserve.

Drain reserved shellfish and mix with softened herb butter. Fill snail shells with mixture, reserving about 4 tablespoons. Place filled sea snails in ovenproof dish and bake in preheated oven for 5 minutes. Heat reserved mixture over low heat.

To serve: In center of each of 4 large oyster plates (with indentations) place a large spoonful of lettuce-tomato mixture; spoon smaller portions in six surrounding indentations. Sprinkle some heated shellfish mixture in center of each plate and place 6 filled sea snail shells in indentations.

Makes 4 servings

A dish of the sea from Alain Chapel: cooked winkles, clams, cockles, and crabs are mixed with softened herb butter and stuffed inside sea snail shells like escargots.

Overleaf: Alain Chapel surrounds sea bass with salsify and shrimp.

Alain Chapel

TRANCHE DE BAR ROTI,
SALSIFIS ET CREVETTES GRISES
AU THYM CITRON, UNE SAUCE ACIDULEE

ROASTED SEA BASS WITH SALSIFY AND SHRIMP

3½	tablespoons olive oil
2	carrots, finely chopped
1	onion, finely chopped
1	leek, well washed and finely chopped
2	ribs celery, finely chopped
4	lobster carcasses, cut into pieces
1	tablespoon Cognac
2	cups dry white wine
2	cups water
1	small head garlic
2	ripe tomatoes, quartered
8	sprigs parsley
	Salt
	Pinch of coarsely cracked black pepper
2	tablespoons lemon juice
¾	cup plus 1½ tablespoons flour
1¼	pounds salsify (oyster plant)
5	sprigs lemon thyme
3	tablespoons balsamic vinegar
2	sea bass (1⅓ pounds each), head and tail removed, dressed, and halved crosswise
	Freshly ground pepper
6	tablespoons cold unsalted butter
½	pound cooked baby shrimp

In a large stockpot, heat 2 tablespoons olive oil. Add carrots, onion, leek, celery, and lobster shells and cook over medium heat, stirring constantly, for about 7 minutes or until vegetables are soft and fragrant. Deglaze briefly with Cognac. Add wine, water, garlic, tomatoes, parsley, a pinch of salt, and cracked black pepper. Stir well and bring to a boil. Reduce heat and simmer for 1 hour.

Meanwhile, in a medium saucepan of salted water, combine lemon juice and 1½ tablespoons flour. Peel salsify and rinse well under cold water. Slice salsify on the diagonal and drop slices into saucepan as you cut them. Bring to a boil over medium-high heat.

62

Reduce heat and simmer for about 12 minutes or until salsify is just tender. Drain in a colander under cold water and set aside.

Strain simmered stock through a fine-mesh strainer set over a saucepan, pressing hard on the solids to extract as much liquid as possible. Boil stock over high heat, skimming as necessary, for about 35 minutes or until reduced to 1 cup. Add 1 sprig thyme and set aside to infuse for 5 minutes. Discard thyme and add balsamic vinegar; set aside.

Preheat oven to 375 degrees. Rinse bass under cold water and pat dry with paper towels. Brush with remaining olive oil and season on both sides with salt and pepper. Flour bass lightly, dusting off any excess. Place bass in a lightly oiled earthenware baking dish and roast in preheated oven, turning once, for about 20 minutes or until the fish is nicely browned and just flakes when pierced with a knife.

Meanwhile, melt 2 tablespoons butter in a large skillet. Add salsify and sauté over medium-high heat, tossing frequently, for about 5 minutes or until lightly browned. Add shrimp.

To serve: Bring sauce to a boil over high heat. Remove from heat and whisk in remaining butter, 1 tablespoon at a time. Reheat salsify and shrimp for about 2 minutes or until warmed through. Pour sauce onto 4 plates and top with roasted bass. Surround fish with salsify and shrimp and garnish each serving with a sprig of lemon thyme.

Makes 4 servings

Alain Chapel

SAINT-PIERRE AU PLAT ET AU FOUR,
COMME UNE SURPRISE

JOHN DORY FILLETS BAKED AS "SURPRISE"

FISH FUMET:

1	tablespoon unsalted butter
1	tablespoon chopped shallots
¼	cup chopped carrots
¼	cup chopped onions
	Bones from 2 whole John Dory, washed, drained, and roughly chopped
2½	cups cold water

The "surprise" of Alain Chapel's John Dory fillets comes from baking them on a bed of onions for a couple of minutes.

JOHN DORY FILLETS:

2	whole John Dory (1½ to 2 pounds each), cut into fillets, or substitute porgy or sole
7	tablespoons unsalted butter Salt and freshly ground pepper
16	small, firm yellow or new potatoes, peeled and sliced ¼-inch thick
1½	cups delicate chicken stock, hot, plus ¼ cup chicken stock, warmed
12	to 16 green onion tops, chopped
4	sprigs fresh thyme or lemon thyme
8	small sprigs fresh basil

Prepare fish fumet: In a heavy enamel or stainless-steel saucepan, melt butter. Add shallots, carrots, and onions and cook until soft, but not browned. Add fish bones and continue to cook for 3 to 5 minutes. Cover with cold water and simmer, skimming surface occasionally, for 20 minutes. Strain and return to a clean, heavy saucepan; cook until reduced to about ½ cup.

Prepare John Dory fillets: Preheat oven to 450 degrees. Wash fish fillets and pat dry with paper towels; reserve in a clean cloth and refrigerate.

Using 1 tablespoon butter for each, grease 4 small gratin dishes; add salt and pepper to taste. Decoratively arrange thin layers of potatoes (3 layers at most) on bottom of each dish. Moisten with 1½ cups hot chicken stock and bake in preheated oven for about 10 minutes or until potatoes are just cooked, but still firm. In a heavy saucepan, melt 1 tablespoon butter. Add green onion tops and cook over low heat until onions are softened, but still firm. Remove potatoes from oven and arrange onions in a thin layer in center of each dish.

In a heavy skillet, melt remaining butter. Add fish fillets and sauté over low to medium heat for about 3 minutes on each side or until fish is cooked, but still firm. Place fillets over onions in each dish and baste with a little butter from skillet. Garnish with thyme and basil, and moisten with 3 tablespoons fish fumet, remaining chicken stock, and some liquid from potatoes. Return to preheated oven and cook for 1 to 2 minutes; serve immediately.

Makes 4 servings

Roger Vergé

LE BLANC DE TURBOT EN MOUSSELINE DE COING

WHITE OF TURBOT IN QUINCE MOUSSELINE

3   to 4 large, very ripe quinces, peeled, halved, and cored
½   cup water
     Salt and freshly ground pepper
2   tablespoons unsalted butter plus 2 tablespoons butter, clarified
2½ pounds turbot, skinned, boned, and cut into 6 thin fillets, or substitute other white saltwater fish
6   young, tender bay leaves, trimmed with pinking shears
2   to 3 cups heavy cream
¼   cup fresh parsley leaves
¼   cup fresh chervil leaves
10 fresh tarragon leaves

Preheat oven to 375 degrees. With a sharp knife, cut quinces into 24 very thin slices. Chop remaining quinces. In a heavy saucepan, combine chopped quinces, water, and a pinch of salt. Cook until soft. Transfer mixture to a food processor, add 2 tablespoons butter, and purée (you should have about 3 cups). Reserve.

In a large ovenproof dish, arrange fish fillets. Place 4 quince slices and a bay leaf on each fillet and salt to taste. Add enough heavy cream to cover fish and bake in preheated oven for about 8 minutes or until fish is very white.

Remove from oven and strain cooking liquid into a small, heavy saucepan; leave just enough liquid in dish to keep fish from becoming dry; cover with aluminum foil and keep warm.

Bring cream to a boil and, whisking constantly, add ¼ cup quince purée. Remove from heat and place in blender with parsley, chervil, and tarragon. Blend until sauce becomes velvety and light green in color. Keep warm.

To serve: Spoon a thin layer of quince purée and a

thin layer of herb sauce to cover the bottom of 6 warmed plates. Place a fish fillet on each plate. With a brush dipped in melted butter, brush surface of fish to remove all traces of cream.

Makes 6 servings

Ed. Note: To give fish a nice white color, place fillets in a large bowl and cover completely with a quart of cold milk, a few ice cubes, and a little water, if necessary. Refrigerate for at least 2 hours; drain just before cooking.

Roger Vergé

LES FLEURS DE COURGETTE AUX TRUFFES

ZUCCHINI FLOWERS STUFFED WITH WHOLE TRUFFLES

4 tablespoons unsalted butter, plus 1 cup cold butter, cut into pieces
1 tablespoon shallot, minced
1 pound very white mushrooms, rinsed, dried, finely chopped, and sprinkled with 1 tablespoon fresh lemon juice
Salt and freshly ground pepper
¼ cup plus 1 tablespoon heavy cream
2 egg yolks
6 tiny zucchini, flowers attached, or substitute pumpkin flowers with pistils removed, blanched Swiss chard, or green cabbage leaves
6 fresh black Vaucluse truffles (½ ounce each), or substitute preserved truffles and reserve juice
1 pound young, tender spinach or mâche, washed and thick stems removed
Fresh chervil leaves, optional

In a heavy saucepan, melt 4 tablespoons butter over medium heat. Add shallots, mushrooms, and salt to taste. Cook, mixing with a wooden spatula, for 3 to 4 minutes. Strain mushrooms through a stainless mesh strainer or cheesecloth; reserve liquid. Return mushrooms to saucepan and cook over medium to high heat for about 3 minutes or until they lose their moisture. Remove from heat and reserve.

In a mixing bowl, whisk together heavy cream and egg yolks. Pour over mushrooms and mix well. Place mixture in a small saucepan and cook over low heat for about 2 minutes; season to taste and spoon into a bowl to cool.

Gently open petals of zucchini flowers, spread a little mushroom mixture inside, and place a truffle in the middle of each flower. (Or spread mushroom mixture on blanched chard or cabbage leaves, top with truffles, and wrap into small packages.) Place zucchini on a small rack and reserve.

In a small, heavy saucepan, combine reserved mushroom juice and any truffle juice. Reduce over medium to high heat until only 3 tablespoons liquid remain. Over medium heat, whisk in cold butter, 2 tablespoons at a time, and add salt and pepper to taste; reserve and keep warm.

Steam filled zucchini for about 15 minutes or until tender.

To serve: Divide spinach or mâche among 6 large plates and arrange zucchini on top. Coat with a little reserved mushroom-truffle sauce and decorate with chervil leaves, if desired.

Makes 6 servings

Roger Vergé's turbot fillets are baked with quince slices and a bay leaf in heavy cream.

Overleaf: Roger Vergé fills the zucchini blossom— still attached to the zucchini—with chopped mushrooms and truffles.

Roger Vergé

LE FILET DE CHEVREUIL, SAUCE POIVRADE FRAMBOISEE

FILLET OF VENISON WITH RED WINE AND RASPBERRIES

3	tablespoons olive oil
1	onion, finely chopped
2	carrots, finely chopped
1	rib celery, finely chopped
4	cloves garlic, finely chopped
7	tablespoons red wine vinegar
1	bottle Côte-Rôtie, Pommard, or Bandol
1	large bouquet garni made with 2 bay leaves, 1 bunch thyme, and 1 bunch parsley stems, tied with string
2	tablespoons coarsely cracked black pepper
8	juniper berries
2¼	pounds lean venison fillet
1	teaspoon tomato paste
½	pint fresh raspberries

1½	tablespoons cornstarch
½	cup plus 1 tablespoon unsalted butter Salt and freshly ground pepper
1	teaspoon red currant jelly
2	tablespoons heavy cream

Heat olive oil in a large casserole. Add the onion, carrots, celery, and garlic and cook over medium heat, stirring frequently for about 15 minutes or until vegetables begin to brown. Add vinegar and bring to a boil over high heat; simmer for about 3 minutes or until liquid reduces to 1 tablespoon. Add wine, bouquet garni, pepper, and juniper berries and return to a boil. Simmer over medium heat for 20 minutes. Remove from heat and let marinade cool completely. (You can transfer marinade to another casserole to speed up cooling.)

Set venison fillet on a rack and place rack in casserole with marinade. Marinate, turning the meat from time to time, for 6 to 8 hours in a cool place, or overnight in the regrigerator. (If meat is refrigerated, bring it to room temperature before roasting.)

Remove venison from marinade and dry well with paper towels. Add tomato paste to marinade and cook over medium-high heat for about 8 minutes or until liquid reduces to 1 cup; set marinade aside.

Preheat oven to 425 degrees. Purée half the raspberries through a fine-mesh strainer. In a small bowl, combine cornstarch with enough wine or water to form a thin paste.

Set a roasting pan over medium-high heat and add 2 tablespoons butter. Season venison with salt and pepper. When butter stops foaming, add meat and sear for about 2 minutes, just until browned on all sides. Transfer venison to oven and roast for 15 to 20 minutes or until quite rare. (At 15 minutes, venison will be very rare; at 20 it will be rare to medium. If you prefer it better done, roast longer. Keep in mind that the meat will continue to cook after it is removed from the oven.) Remove meat from roasting pan, cover with aluminum foil, and set aside.

Meanwhile, prepare sauce. Drain fat from roasting pan and add reserved marinade. Set pan over medium heat and stir with a wooden spoon, scraping bottom to dislodge and dissolve any roasting juices. Strain mixture through a fine mesh strainer set over a medium saucepan; press hard on the solids to extract all juices. Stir in raspberry purée.

Set saucepan over medium heat and whisk in liquefied cornstarch, a little at a time, until sauce is of desired consistency. (You may not need to use all the cornstarch.) Whisk in remaining butter, one tablespoon at a time. Stir in red currant jelly and season with salt and pepper to taste. In a small bowl, combine ¼ cup sauce and heavy cream.

To serve: Slice meat and arrange on 6 heated plates. Grind fresh pepper over meat and ladle some sauce over each serving. Top with a little cream sauce and, with a fork, marble the two sauces together. Garnish with remaining raspberries. Pass remaining sauce in sauceboat.

Makes 6 servings

Ed. note: The chef serves this dish with chestnut purée and small pears poached in red wine.

Chef's Note: Many people enjoy the sauces that accompany game dishes but are not too fond of the meat itself; such is the case with me. The sauce for this dish could be used with any other good cut of venison, as well as with a beef tenderloin or a leg of lamb. If fresh raspberries are unavailable, as they often are during game season, you can use flash-frozen raspberries instead.

Louis Outhier

LANGOUSTES AUX HERBES THAI
ROCK LOBSTER WITH THAI HERBS

71

2	rock lobsters (2 pounds each), or substitute lobsters
2	tablespoons unsalted butter
1	teaspoon dried green and red hot peppers or peppery curry powder
2	leaves lemongrass, cut into thin strips
1	teaspoon minced shallots
2	tablespoons grated ginger
2	carrots, peeled, cut into long, thin strips, or grated
2	Golden Delicious apples, cut into long, thin strips
¾	cup white port
½	teaspoon turmeric
1	cup heavy cream, whipped
	Salt to taste

(Recipe continued on following page.)

Preceding overleaf: Louis Outhier discovered Asian seasoning when he visited the East; one result is his lobster with Thai herbs.

Left: Filet of venison with red wine and raspberries is another Vergé creation.

Preheat oven to 375 degrees. Place rock lobsters in enough boiling water to cover and poach for 3 minutes; remove and cool. With a sharp knife, cut rock lobsters in half lengthwise and remove flesh. (If using regular lobsters, remove flesh from claws.)

Bake empty lobster shells in preheated oven for 7 to 8 minutes. Remove and reserve.

In a heavy enamel or stainless-steel saucepan, melt butter. Add lobster meat and cook over moderate heat, stirring constantly, for about 2 minutes. Remove from heat and divide evenly among lobster shells. Cover with aluminum foil and keep warm.

In the same saucepan, combine dried peppers, lemongrass, and shallots. Cook over high heat for about 1 minute. Add ginger, carrots, apples, port, and turmeric and continue to cook over high heat until liquid reduces to a glaze. Add cream and salt to taste; stir and return to a boil.

Spoon sauce over each lobster half and serve.

Makes 4 servings

Louis Outhier

MILLEFEUILLE DE SAUMON AU CERFEUIL

SALMON MILLEFEUILLE WITH CHERVIL

3/4   pound puff pastry, fresh or frozen, rolled into a 17-by-14-inch rectangle

1   tablespoon plus 1 teaspoon unsalted butter

1   teaspoon finely minced shallots

1/2   cup dry white wine

1   cup heavy cream
    Salt and cayenne pepper to taste

1   pound fresh salmon, sliced 1/16- to 1/8-inch thick

1/4   cup fresh chervil leaves, finely chopped

72

Preheat oven to 425 degrees.

Sprinkle a 17-by-14-inch baking sheet with water. Place puff pastry on baking sheet and prick well with a fork; cover with a rack to impede rising. Bake in preheated oven for 15 minutes, then reduce temperature to 350 degrees and cook 10 to 15 minutes longer.

Meanwhile, prepare sauce. In a small, heavy saucepan, melt 1 tablespoon butter over low heat. Add shallots and cook until softened but not colored. Add wine and reduce over medium heat until liquid evaporates, but shallots remain wet. Add cream, salt, and cayenne. Boil for 4 minutes or until thickened. Remove from heat and keep warm.

With a serrated knife, cut puff pastry into 4 equal rectangles, each about ¼-inch wide. Keep warm.

In a large, heavy, nonstick skillet, melt 1 teaspoon butter. Add salmon and cook over medium heat for about 2 seconds on each side.

Start with a rectangle of pastry and alternate layers of salmon and pastry until the ingredients are all used. Top with a layer of pastry. Trim the millefeuille with a serrated knife and divide it into four servings.

Arrange the millefeuilles on heated plates and spoon sauce over the top and around the bottom of the pastry. Sprinkle each serving with chervil.

Makes 4 servings

Michel Guérard

LA CORONE D'ABONDANCE AUX FRUITS GLACES

HORN OF PLENTY WITH GLAZED FRUITS

PASTRY AND GLAZED FRUITS:
- ¼ pound puff pastry, fresh or frozen
- ¼ cup flour
- 1 tablespoon powdered sugar
- 1 kiwi, peeled and quartered
- ½ mango, peeled and cut into 4 pieces
- 1 pear, peeled and quartered
- 8 whole strawberries, leaves and stems intact

CHANTILLY CREAM:
- 1 cup heavy cream, chilled
- 2 tablespoons powdered sugar
- ½ teaspoon vanilla extract

RASPBERRY COULIS:
- 1 cup fresh raspberries plus 20 perfect raspberries, for garnish
- ½ cup water
- ⅓ cup granulated sugar
- ½ lemon, juiced

ASSEMBLY:
- 4 tiny bunches white grapes (3 to 4 grapes each)
- 4 tiny bunches red grapes (3 to 4 grapes each)
- 4 sprigs mint
- 4 sprigs verbena
- ½ pint pistachio ice cream

73

(Recipe continued on following page.)

Millefeuille is an utterly French invention. Louis Outhier's salmon millefeuille combines shallots with the salmon in a cream-and-white-wine sauce.

Prepare pastry and glazed fruits: Preheat oven to 400 degrees. On a lightly floured work surface, roll out pastry to a 5-by-16-inch rectangle that is 1/16-inch thick. With a sharp knife, cut four 1¼-by-16-inch bands. Butter four 2-by-2¼-inch cornets and beginning at the pointed end, wrap 1 band of pastry around each; work toward open end in a spiral pattern. Press any extra pastry inside horn. Sprinkle with powdered sugar and place on a moistened, metal baking sheet. Bake in preheated oven for about 20 minutes or until nut brown in color. Remove from oven and cool on a rack.

Slice kiwi, mango, and pear pieces into fan shapes. Set aside.

Prepare Chantilly cream: In a medium bowl set over a bowl of ice, combine cream, sugar, and vanilla and whip until soft peaks form.

Prepare raspberry coulis: In a blender or food processor, purée 1 cup raspberries. Strain purée into a bowl. In a small, heavy saucepan, combine water and sugar. Cook over medium heat for about 4 minutes or until sugar is melted and mixture forms a slightly thickened light syrup. Remove from heat and set aside to cool. In a medium bowl, combine raspberry purée, cooled syrup, and lemon juice. Refrigerate.

To serve: With a sharp serrated knife, remove pastry horns from molds. Fill each with 1 tablespoon Chantilly cream. Place a cream-filled horn at the top of each of 4 chilled plates. Spoon 3 tablespoons Raspberry Coulis in front of each horn. Place sliced (fanned) fruits on coulis and dip strawberries and reserved raspberries into remaining coulis to glaze. Garnish plates with grapes, glazed berries, mint sprigs, and verbena. Place a small scoop of ice cream in the opening of each horn and serve immediately.

Makes 4 servings

Michel Guérard

LES RAVIOLES DE TRUFFES A LA CREME DE MOUSSERONS

TRUFFLE RAVIOLI WITH WILD MUSHROOM CREAM SAUCE

FRESH RAVIOLI DOUGH:
- 1 cup unbleached flour
- 1 large egg
- 1 large egg yolk
- ¼ teaspoon salt
- 1 tablespoon olive oil
- 1 to 1½ tablespoons water

MUSHROOM DUXELLES:
- ½ cup unsalted butter
- ⅓ cup finely chopped shallots
- ¾ pound very white mushrooms, chopped as finely as possible, without puréeing, and sprinkled with 2 tablespoons lemon juice
- 1 tablespoon white wine
- ¼ teaspoon finely chopped garlic
- ¼ teaspoon salt
- ⅛ teaspoon freshly ground pepper
- 1 tablespoon flour
- ½ cup crème fraîche

WILD MUSHROOM CREAM SAUCE:
- ½ pound mousserons (St. George's Agaric) or other fresh, delicate, savory wild mushrooms, rinsed and dried
- ⅓ cup truffle juice, optional
- 2 cups heavy cream
- 1 cup unsalted butter
  Salt and freshly ground pepper

ASSEMBLY:
- 1 ounce fresh or preserved truffle, cut into 18 thin slices
  Fresh chervil

Michel Guérard fills his tender raviolis with truffles, mushroom, and shallots.

Overleaf: The secret of Michel Guérard's elegant dessert of glazed fruits is its careful assembly.

Prepare ravioli dough: In a food processor, combine flour, egg, egg yolk, salt, and olive oil. Process for a few seconds. Add 1 tablespoon water and process, adding 1 to 2 teaspoons additional water, for a few seconds or until dough forms a ball. Wrap dough in plastic wrap and refrigerate for 4 to 6 hours.

Prepare mushroom duxelles: In a heavy saucepan, melt butter over medium heat. Add shallots and cook until they are soft and free of moisture. Add mushrooms, wine, garlic, salt, and pepper and continue to cook until moisture has evaporated; mixture should not brown. Add flour and continue to cook over low heat, stirring with a wooden spoon, for 2 minutes. Remove from heat and cool. Stir in crème fraîche, cover, and refrigerate.

Prepare wild mushroom cream sauce: In a small, heavy saucepan, combine wild mushrooms, truffle juice, and heavy cream. Heat over medium heat for 3 to 5 minutes. Stir in butter, a few pieces at a time, and season with salt and pepper to taste. Remove from heat and set aside.

Assemble ravioli and serve: On a floured work surface, roll out ravioli dough as thinly as possible. With a 3-inch cookie cutter, cut dough into 36 rounds. In center of 18 dough rounds, place 1 teaspoon duxelles mixture, a slice of truffle, and another teaspoon duxelles mixture. With a brush dipped in water, moisten edges of ravioli dough and place another round on top; press edges to seal well.

In a large pot, bring 2 quarts water to a boil. Add ½ teaspoon salt. Add ravioli and poach for 6 to 10 minutes. Remove with a slotted spoon and refresh in cold water. Drain and set ravioli aside on a clean, dry cloth.

In a large, heavy saucepan, reheat ravioli with wild mushroom cream sauce. Spoon some sauce into bottom of several heated dishes, add 2 to 3 ravioli to each, and decorate with chervil.

Makes 6 to 9 servings

Michel Guérard

LES ECREVISSES CUITES A L'ETOUFFEE EN MARINIERE DE LEGUMES

SMOTHERED CRAYFISH WITH BABY VEGETABLES

4	small red potatoes
8	cloves garlic, unpeeled, plus 1 clove garlic, peeled and finely chopped
4	shallots, unpeeled
	Salt
	Sugar
4	baby carrots with tops
4	baby turnips with tops
4	spring onions with tops
4	small leeks, well washed
4	pounds fresh mussels, scrubbed and debearded
¼	cup dry white wine
5½	pounds live crayfish, well rinsed
	Bouquet garni
6	large fresh basil leaves
1	tablespoon olive oil
7	tablespoons unsalted butter
	Freshly ground pepper
1	tablespoon finely chopped parsley
	Fresh chervil leaves

78

In a medium saucepan, combine potatoes, unpeeled garlic cloves, and shallots. Cover with cold water, salt lightly, and bring to a boil over high heat. Reduce heat to medium and cook for about 15 minutes or until potatoes are barely tender. Drain, discard garlic and shallots, and set aside.

In a saucepan of salted, lightly sugared water, combine carrots, turnips, and onions. Bring to a boil and cook over medium-high heat for about 10 minutes or until vegetables are barely tender. Drain and refresh under cold water.

Cook leeks in boiling salted water for about 4 minutes or until just tender.

Place mussels in a large saucepan. Cover and cook over high heat, shaking pan occasionally, for about 7 minutes or until mussels open. Transfer mussels to a bowl and reserve for another use. Strain cooking liquid and reserve (you should have about 2 cups).

In a large, heavy casserole, arrange all cooked vegetables. Moisten with mussel liquid and wine and bring to a boil. Add crayfish and bouquet garni, cover, and cook over medium-high heat for 5 minutes. Set casserole aside and let steam for 2 minutes longer.

Meanwhile, purée basil leaves and olive oil in a food processor.

To serve: Remove crayfish and arrange on 4 large plates. With a slotted spoon, remove vegetables from casserole and place one of each on each plate.

Add basil purée and chopped garlic to casserole and bring to a boil over high heat. Cook for about 10 minutes or until liquid is reduced to 1¼ cups. Remove from heat and whisk in butter, 1 tablespoon at a time. Season with salt and pepper to taste and strain through a fine-mesh strainer. Stir in parsley and spoon some sauce over each serving. Sprinkle with chervil and serve immediately.

Makes 4 servings

Crayfish and baby vegetables are combined colorfully by Michel Guérard.

TODAY'S INNOVATORS

SINCE THE ARRIVAL OF BOCUSE, Troisgros, and the other founding fathers of modern cuisine, a new generation of chefs now in their late twenties and early thirties is quickly growing up behind them, impatient for a turn in the limelight. This explosion of culinary talent burst forth four or five years ago, and it gives no sign of losing momentum.

These men and (occasionally) women are the innovators of today. Having learned from the successes as well as the failures of their nouvelle cuisine predecessors, they have discovered a balance that includes both past and present. They reject the worst of the modern school's eccentricities, without falling back on the grande cuisine of yesteryear. Their inspiration comes partly from the repertory of regional specialties, which they lighten and modernize, but, above all, they explore, they invent, they create. Some of these cooks have not only caught up with the elders of their craft: they have also outstripped many of them in terms of celebrity and sheer talent.

Obviously, not all are on the same level. Some have reached master status, like Alain Senderens, Joël Robuchon, Jacques Maximin, and Marc Meneau. Others, like Michel and Jean-Michel Lorain, Jean Bardet, Bernard Loiseau, Pierre Gagnaire, Michel Bras, Guy Savoy, or Alain Dutournier, are fast approaching that rank. Still others are moving forward rapidly. The forty chefs discussed on the following tour are absolutely the crème de la crème.

In France, everything starts in Paris, and so shall we. Alain Senderens, the chef at Lucas-Carton, has already been mentioned. He is gaining a reputation in the United States, where he visits regularly. The young chef from southwestern France began his career in a small Left Bank restaurant and has become one of the uncontested masters of French cuisine. His mind fairly teems with ideas, and despite the rare error or lapse, his talent has something of the genius about it. Like Michel Guérard, his name will go down in gastronomic history.

Joël Robuchon is also unquestionably one of the foremost culinary talents of France, indeed, of the world. His charming digs, with their elegant Old World flavor and pink and flowered chintz, are very popular. Reserving a table for dinner there is more difficult than speaking with the President.

Robuchon still has the rustic tastes and the respect for fine ingredients and pure flavors that come from his country childhood, yet he is first and foremost a dazzling creator. A dish that resembles one of his in another restaurant is

Alain Senderens marinates venison in a mixture of red wine, shallots, raspberry vinegar, lime juice, and parsley stems, then roasts it, and serves with juniper butter.

sure to be a copy. Robuchon copies no one; he is an original.

Because he is a consummate artist, a dinner at Robuchon's table is a feast for the eye as well as the palate. Witness the cream of cauliflower with caviar aspic or the peppered lobster with artichoke slivers sautéed in olive oil with a hint of curry; the salt cod with fava beans and soy sauce is as admirable as the simmered pig's head accompanied by the best mashed potatoes to be had; the prawn and cabbage ravioli, the sweetbreads with spinach, the spiced duck, or the roasted lamb in a salt crust are wonderfully delicious. From the crème brûlée to the bitter chocolate cake, desserts prolong the pleasure of this extraordinary state of grace. Robuchon can turn anything, even the simplest salad, into a masterpiece.

Unlike Joël Robuchon, Guy Savoy has not yet had the good fortune to find premises commensurate with his talent. He is obliged to cook in cramped kitchens and to serve his customers in a rather uncomfortable room. But the surroundings don't stop people from crowding into his establishment, for Savoy's cooking makes them forget everything else. All the dishes harmonize with extraordinary grace; the flavors, textures, and aromas are never blurred by needless sauces. On the contrary, they are highlighted by cooking juices, purées, and meat or vegetable essences that give Savoy's cuisine a rare subtlety. To whet the appetite, one might begin with a trio of variations on a theme: poached oysters, oyster mousse, and oyster aspic. Next come small morsels of lobster rolled in spinach leaves, served with snowpeas and a heavenly sauce made with the lobster carcass and coral. Then, on a bed of potatoes, a nearly caramelized filet of monkfish enhanced with a subtle shallot juice that contains neither white wine nor vinegar. Later comes a filet of red mullet sautéed with chicken livers and bitter endive; still later,

Guy Savoy

Alain Dutournier
Le Carré des Feuillants

sweetbreads lightly fried in butter with firm little mushrooms. Finally, chicken breast, just barely caramelized, with fresh fava beans. The grace note is a millefeuille with cloud-light pastry cream. Those dishes are only a few of the oft-renewed array offered by Guy Savoy, who is one of the most imaginative chefs of his generation.

Another member of the same generation is Alain Dutournier, a native of southwest France. He has just left his bistro, Au Trou Gascon, to open a very attractive new restaurant called Le Carré des Feuillants, situated near the Place Vendôme in the courtyard of a historic building that once was the residence of the Countess of Castiglione, a celebrated personality of the Napoleon III era. This young Gascon is equally at ease preparing country dishes that he cleverly lightens and modernizes (roast salmon with smoked bacon, duck breast with preserved turnips, young rabbit sautéed with tiny purple artichokes, duck liver with green asparagus, cassoulet) and contemporary, innovative cuisine, which on his menu he terms "my latest ideas": crab ravioli with basil, red mullet with eggplant caviar, chopped scallops with ginger, sweetbreads poached raw with artichokes and oysters

in a cabbage leaf, or an extraordinary gâteau of eels that is sure to change your thinking about this fish, often considered too fatty. Dutournier's wine list is one of the best and most original in Paris, particularly well stocked with exquisite, relatively inexpensive Bordeaux that are rarely available elsewhere.

Michel Rostang, whose father runs the well-known Bonne Auberge in Antibes, took over the premises formerly occupied by Denis, a great and extravagant chef, now deceased, whose notoriety crossed the Atlantic when he served New York *Times* food critic Craig Claiborne "the world's most expensive meal." Michel Rostang, whose cooking style admirably harmonizes the bourgeois and the modern, turned this charmless setting into one of the most elegant spots in town. You'll spend a delightful evening in this intimate, refined atmosphere, sampling such delicacies as quail's eggs stuffed with sea urchins, sautéed skate with lightly browned butter, a crusty galette of wild salmon, red mullet in a sauce made with their livers and cream, goat cheese ravioli poached in chicken broth, steamed squab stuffed with wild rice and foie gras, or an admirable, totally greaseless pot-au-feu.

Jacques Cagna's inn is located in a ravishing

83

Joël Robuchon's restaurant has an Old World flavor, but there is nothing old fashioned about his cuisine. Many of his fellow chefs regard Robuchon as the most original culinary talent in France.

seventeenth-century Parisian dwelling not far from Notre Dame. It is a jewel among Left Bank restaurants, with its ceiling adorned with great oaken beams and its authentic Flemish paintings and candle-lit tables. The food prepared by this very engaging young chef is modern but unaffected, light without being bland, highlighted by keen, frank flavors. His red mullet with fava beans, thyme, and coriander; his civet of hog's jowls and trotters in red wine; his ravioli with mild garlic purée; the filet of brill with lobster mousse; rib of Scottish beef sautéed with shallots; his duck in Burgundy flavored with lemon and orange zest; and the chocolate and walnut cake are all close to perfection. If there is a last bottle of Côte-Rôtie La Mouline (a great growth from the Côtes-du-Rhône) in the cellar, don't hesitate to order it, for it is a grandiose wine!

Two young Parisian cooks have lately joined the pack of leading chefs. The first, Philippe Groult, worked for nine years with Joël Robuchon. Since his arrival at Le Manoir de Paris, food lovers have been flocking in to sample a cuisine that is reminiscent (but not imitative) of his former mentor's. His cod with anchovies, his sautéed prawns with zucchini, or the braised pork with lentils are all flawless dishes, beautifully presented, that show remarkable finesse and great personality.

The second, Régis Mahé, is a trim young man who came up to the capital after a stint in Nice as assistant to Jacques Maximin and who now presides at Le Bourdonnais. There is a sunny, southern lilt to his cooking, which is light, harmonious, and delicate, with refined and sophisticated flavor combinations (artichoke and foie gras soufflé; jellied daube of duck and pig's trotters; filet of lamb with girolle mushrooms and herbed goat cheese ravioli; a mixed grill of red mullet, sea bream, and sardines all cooked in their skins).

There is a venerable tradition of feminine cookery in France, but it is rare for a female chef to break out of bourgeois cuisine and make a mark with a style of her own. In Paris, Dominique Nahmias is the best of that creative breed. She and her husband, Albert, own a dinner restaurant, Olympe, with a 1930s decor that is a great favorite with show business celebrities. Dominique Nahmias is widely known thanks to her television cooking show, and her very personal, Provençal-inspired culinary style is famous. Her raw sea bream with chives, sauced with a mixture of hazelnut oil, olive oil, and soy sauce; her warm oysters with fresh pasta; the turbot with olive oil, snow peas, bell peppers, and eggplant; her crayfish with artichokes; the smoked sweet-and-sour duck; and her marvelous chocolate fondant are just a few of the remarkable creations dreamed up by this young woman who had planned to study law before the kitchen won the battle for her soul.

Compared with these young chefs, Jacques Le Divellec might seem more like an elder statesman, but the exceptional youthfulness of the man who revolutionized fish cookery belies his fifty-odd years. For two decades, Le Divellec ran the best restaurant in La Rochelle on the Atlantic coast. He recently resettled in Paris near the Quai d'Orsay (the Foreign Affairs Ministry) where he opened an elegant restaurant called, not unexpectedly, Le Divellec. The place has the air of a yacht club and it is always full. Le Divellec has a positive reverence for fish, and no patience for those who destroy its delicate taste by overcooking, overstuffing, or oversaucing it.

That is not to say that he merely sautés or broils fish, then serves it up plain. His special talent is to prepare fish without spoiling its natural flavor, as you will see when you sample his eels, skate, red mullet, and shellfish in court bouillon; the bass roasted in its skin; oysters just barely cooked in sea-fennel; sea bream braised with fennel; or his sautéed turbot with fresh pasta and a chive-flavored sabayon sauce.

Just a few miles from Paris, in an elegant dwelling that stands in the park surrounding Maisons-Laffitte, works another truly creative cook: François Clerc, owner of La Vieille Fontaine. This is Catherine Deneuve's favorite restaurant; she often jumps into her car to come here and indulge in Clerc's "aumonières de caviar" (caviar-filled crêpes); the salmon millefeuille spiced with mustard seeds; skate with sea urchin cream; extraordinary squab pâté rolled up in a "turban" of pasta; seven-hour leg of lamb with buttered creamed cabbage; and all of Clerc's fantastic desserts.

Let's leave the capital now and chart a course for points south, on the road that passes through Burgundy and the Rhône valley, on its way to the Riviera.

Burgundy has always enjoyed an exceptional gastronomic reputation, yet, only ten or fifteen years ago, it was something of a challenge to find a really good restaurant in the region. The same old dishes were on every menu, drowning in heavy, indigestible sauces; even the most time-honored specialties were pretty wretched. The tide began to turn with the rise of nouvelle cuisine. Today, Burgundy is again a stronghold of French gastronomy, envied even by the Lyonnais, ever boastful of their superiority in the culinary sphere.

In Joigny, the old Côte Saint-Jacques has been transformed from a country inn into a ravishing luxury hotel, with sumptuous apartments overlooking the river. Owner Michel Lorain was a chef of the old school, not lacking in talent, but

Jacqueline Lorain holds the beginnings of vintage Burgundy in the family vineyard at Joigny.

inclined to fussiness. Five or six years ago, his style began to evolve, a change that was consolidated when son Jean-Michel joined his father in the kitchen after a training period with Fredy Girardet in Switzerland. Their subtle, intelligent cuisine makes La Côte Saint-Jacques one of the premier tables of France. Their carp aspic; the prawn gazpacho with cream of zucchini; the scallops and foie gras steamed in parchment; the salmon cooked in a bladder; their snails with cream of parsley and tomato fondue; the pigeon with mild garlic and potato cakes; the veal kidney with artichokes and bell peppers; duck with lentils and onions; and their wickedly tempting desserts all point up the perfection the pair has attained in calculating cooking times and harmonizing flavors. Michel Lorain's wife, Jacqueline, is an expert sommelier. She can be trusted to unearth the Meursault or Chambertin of one's dreams.

Marc Meneau's house in Saint-Père-sous-Vézelay, a comfortable middle-class villa, has an enveloping, intimate atmosphere. L'Espérance, as the restaurant is called, is set amid a small park with a stream where wild ducks paddle. His wife, Françoise, a peerless hostess, welcomes guests. Everything here is designed to delight

85

the eye and the spirit: the attractive suites set in an antique mill, the bright and cheerful rooms, the sumptuous breakfasts, beautiful wines, and all around you the green meadows and châteaux of the Burgundy countryside.

Meneau's secret is to ignore fashion, to forget about impressing his colleagues, and to cook only to please himself and his wife. He is a careful craftsman with the soul of an artist. It is hard to decide which is more remarkable, the fertility of his imagination, the natural spontaneity of his style, the freshness of his cuisine, the clarity of the sauces, or the accuracy of the proportions and seasoning. Emotionally rooted to the land, Meneau conveys the flavors and smells of the surrounding countryside in every aspect of his cuisine: the tiny, light pâté meat balls that contain a nearly liquid filling of foie gras; the assortment of garden vegetables in fragrant chicken bouillon; the fabulous lobster with olive oil, garnished with an exquisite fennel purée; the duck liver that is nearly caramelized in mushroom cooking juices; the filet of red mullet with watercress; his whole turbot roasted in its skin and served with onions cooked in meat juices (the match of the century!); plump and tender Loire salmon with potato straws; his stewed-rabbit tart; the truffled filet of roasted veal with artichokes; the double chocolate (one solid, one liquid) soufflé; the cherry vanilla ice cream; his walnut crème brûlée; or the fantastic pineapple millefeuille. You leave the table feeling so light that you are almost tempted to start in again!

Before World War II, and up until the 1960s, Alexander Dumaine's inn, La Côte d'Or in Saulieu, was a compulsory stopping place on the road leading from Lyons to the Riviera. Celebrities from the world over visited there, but decline set in after Dumaine's retirement. The house was in a deplorable state when young Bernard Loiseau decided to settle there a few years ago. The renovation effort is not yet complete, but with his wife, Chantal, Bernard has put in some charming suites above the newly landscaped garden. La Côte d'Or is now one of the most pleasant stopping places in Burgundy.

Bernard Loiseau is a genuinely creative chef, with a passion for innovation. He has practically banished heavy sauces from his kitchen, going so far as to use water as the liquid in some of his reductions, a technique that is not to everyone's liking. Especially memorable are a very simple but admirable vegetable fricassée fragrant with chervil; his red mullet with artichokes; "water roasted" lobster; snails with nettle butter; sea bream in red wine with shallot marmelade; braised leg of rabbit with cabbage; veal sweetbreads and kidneys with girolle mushrooms and leeks so tiny that Loiseau must have used tweezers to pull them from the garden. Outstanding wines to be sampled are Jean-Noël Gagnard's Bâtard-Montrachet, the Beaune Vignes Franches from Jacques Germain, or Simon Bize's Santenay.

Marc Meneau, a chef with the soul of an artist, cooks to please himself and his wife.

Our next halt is Lameloise, in Chagny. There is no garden or birdsong to greet the guest at the old Lameloise family hotel, set in the center of a little town surrounded by vineyards, but the civilized pleasures of an elegant, old-fashioned decor, a warm and courteous reception, and sumptuous breakfasts more than compensate. The culinary pleasures are compliments of young Jacques Lameloise, who has taken over from his father, Jean, in the kitchen and has given a new direction to the classic house repertory. Be sure to try the terrine of young rabbit with fresh mint; his frogs sautéed with mild garlic; his herbed crayfish aspic; the Bresse squab cooked in a bladder, accompanied by fresh pasta with foie gras, and then finish up with strawberry millefeuille. There to advise on wine is Georges Pertuiset, one of the most knowledgeable sommeliers in France.

Georges Blanc is as accomplished a restaurateur as he is a chef. He has transformed an utterly ordinary family inn in Vonnas, La mère Blanc—where fifty years ago his grandmother's cooking was famed throughout the region—into

one of the loveliest stopovers in France. The spacious dining room with rough stone walls is decorated with a graceful Louis XIV tapestry and immense bouquets of fresh flowers. One hundred diners are all served with the same attention and courtesy. The service never allows of a false note; each meal is an exercise in faultless harmony.

Georges Blanc scours the countryside and the farms of Bresse for the local chickens, pigeons, ducks, frogs, vegetables, and herbs that give his cooking its incomparable freshness and savor. Unlike some of his peers, Blanc stubbornly refuses to abandon his kitchens; that probably explains the precision and consistency of a cuisine that is highly sophisticated despite its apparent simplicity, a skillful mix of contemporary tastes and regional traditions.

The tomato and foie gras slipped into a simple soft-boiled egg make a surprising but savory combination. The warm frogs' legs salad with chives is judiciously seasoned with a dash of vinegar. A cold casserole of crayfish claws and tails takes on a new, disarming flavor thanks to a lemony herb sauce. Traditional potato pancakes are made sublime with the addition of smoked salmon and caviar. Don't miss the tomato stuffed with snails, sauced with an unexpected blend of herbs and white wine; the chicken liver ravioli in a highly spiced sauce made with sparkling Burgundy wine; or the casseroled Bresse chicken flanked by vegetables so fresh that they taste almost unfamiliar. Georges Blanc's lamb chops are incomparable. He marinates them for two days in garlic and olive oil, then cooks them in a lamb and veal stock thickened with butter. Magnificent. And nobody makes a better coffee meringue. All his desserts, in fact, are brilliant. The same goes for the wines, chosen by one of France's best "noses,"

The charm of the Burgundy countryside surrounds Meneau's inn, L'Esperance.

Marcel Périnet, who is assisted by a young English sommelier, Peter William Lowe.

Moving south, we arrive in Lyons, a rather insular city, greatly attached to its traditional gastronomy. Yet two young chefs have recently managed to introduce a somewhat different style, and their restaurants are definitely worth a visit. The first is Jean-Paul Lacombe, who succeeded his father in the kitchens of a venerable bistro loaded with charm, Léon de Lyon. Miraculously, this polished young man is just as adept at preparing the classic Lyonnais repertory (much lightened) as he is at cooking in a far more modern and personal register. He switches from one to another with remarkable flair: from the tripe with tomatoes to the terrine of foie gras and artichoke bottoms, from the traditional pike mousse to the exquisite red mullet and fennel in aspic, or from the sauté of lamb with fava beans to a delicate pink grapefruit terrine. And along with all these dishes, served in a dining room decorated with paintings and kitchen utensils that seem to belong to another age, can

88

be drunk the best Beaujolais on earth.

Lyons' other young innovator is thirty-year-old Philippe Chavent, established at the stoves of one of the loveliest Renaissance houses in old Lyons: La Tour Rose. It took some doing to convince the natives of Lyons that red mullet sautéed with bacon and curry, or stewed oysters (or sweetbreads) with puréed dried peas seasoned with a dash of orange pulp could be good to eat, but Chavent has managed to do so.

Saint-Etienne (located about thirty-five miles southwest of Lyons) would seem too quiet were it not the home of one of today's most fascinating young talents, Pierre Gagnaire. His restaurant is a former photographer's studio, renovated with the help of his German wife, Gabrielle. They converted it into a handsome, New York-style loft, with lacquered woodwork in strong colors, modern paintings, and a veritable forest of plants. Although he is not yet widely known, Gagnaire personifies the contemporary creative chef. He nimbly skirts all the pitfalls of "fashionable" cuisine, for he is a cook of rare subtlety. His imagination is so lively that after proposing a whole menu, he may well serve something entirely different concocted on a moment's inspiration! At any rate, nothing he makes resembles what you may find in other restaurants. Witness his prawns in beet juice with stewed zucchini; the gâteau of artichokes; his compote of beef jowls with turnips and snowpeas seasoned with rapeseed oil; or sliced roast lobster with fava beans in a cinnamon- and chervil-flavored butter. Or try his curried veal sauté with zucchini and bell peppers, garnished with sweetbread croquettes and spinach with truffles; the salmi of wild duck braised in a bouillon of sautéed artichokes; or, finally, his fantastic hot, warm, or cold "chocolate soup." There is still not much risk of running into many foreign

Diners enjoy a late afternoon meal at Bernard Loiseau's Hôtel de la Côte d'Or on the road to the Riviera.

tourists at Pierre Gagnaire's place, but he may do for Saint-Etienne what the Troisgros did for Roanne!

If we cross back over the Rhône River, we find ourselves in Valence. It is not quite Provence, but the quality of the light lets you know that it is not far away. It would be absurd to make Jacques Pic out to be either a young man or an innovator. Yet ever since he took over the family restaurant, made famous by his father in the 1950s, he has given the food a new tone that contrasts vividly with the rather discreet charm of this opulent provincial house, dear to the hearts of the area's notables. The truffles (admirable, locally grown) with turnips, the red mullet salad with asparagus, the mixed grill of bass and salmon in parsley sauce, the warm lobster with minced vegetables and sherry are certainly not the sort of thing one could find in the fifties! They are perfectly modern, and perfectly delicious; beneath Pic's unassuming exterior hides the heart of a great and subtle cook. His assortment of desserts is a masterpiece. Chez Pic, forget about Burgundies and Bordeaux; choose instead from among the lordly Côtes-du-Rhône, such as the white or red Hermitages, or the Châteauneuf-du-Pape. After you taste these sumptuous wines, you are sure to wonder why the French know so little about them.

At the foot of the stunning village perched on a cliff called Les Baux, in a strange, dreamlike landscape bathed in the limpid atmosphere of Provence, stands L'Oustau de Baumanière. In the fifties and sixties it was a sanctuary of French gastronomy. Then, despite Raymond Thulier's phenomenal vitality (he is now eighty-six), this sumptuous inn began to show signs of lassitude. But now Thulier's grandson, Jean-André Charial, who trained in the Troisgros kitchens, has reenergized the Oustau. With the

help of chef Alain Burnel, the young man has put all his efforts into refurbishing the cuisine, with the sunny flavors and accents of Provence. The food is rustic, yet amazingly refined: filets of red mullet cooked in red wine, served on a bed of leeks; lobster with ratatouille; herb-stuffed rabbit; charlotte of lamb with eggplant; salmon with olives; frozen nougat with strawberry purée; and hot mint soufflé with chocolate sauce.

Ten years ago, gastronomy was wasting away on the Riviera. Except Roger Vergé and Louis Outhier, there wasn't another great cook between Saint Tropez and Monte Carlo. But these days, there is an explosion of young culinary talent on the coast. If a single one were to be given special attention, it would have to be Jacques Maximin. At thirty-five, he is one of the new stars of French cuisine. As of this writing, he does not yet have his own place, but he may soon leave the Chantecler, the restaurant of the Negresco, an old luxury hotel, to open a restaurant of his own near Nice. Though the Negresco puts considerable means at Maximin's disposal,

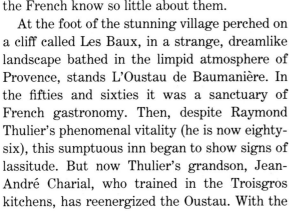

The Mediterranean resort of Cannes draws a fashionable crowd to its beaches.

the Chantecler dining room is devoid of charm, lacking in elegance, and can only be viewed as a handicap. Wherever Maximin eventually lands, you must seek out this small, dark, nervous young man who has been dubbed "the Bonaparte of the kitchen." He has a prodigious creative gift, perhaps even a touch of genius. No one has turned the Provençal culinary heritage to better account: he has created a cuisine that is innovative yet true to its roots.

It was Maximin, for example, who launched the craze for stuffed zucchini blossoms, now imitated all over the world. But the list of his creations, each more dazzling than the next, is too long to enumerate. Although no preparation stays on the menu for long—it is perpetually renewed and revised—several must be mentioned: the lobster infused with truffle juice; the foie gras in Sauternes aspic with asparagus tips; the chopped scallops in a shallot-and-truffle butter; pigeon soup with lentils and marrow; the garlic-scented duck with a gratin of turnips and prunes; the rabbit gratinéed with mushrooms. For desserts there is his rum-flavored macaroon

or the frozen nougat with raspberry sauce.

Maximin's fantastic success has encouraged other inventive young chefs, who are liable to become great names in their own right. In Cannes, Jacques Chibois is causing sparks to fly at Le Royal-Gray, the restaurant of the Hôtel Gray d'Albion, where he serves an elegant cuisine with a Provençal accent, free of mannerisms and tics. A little older, but just as brilliant as Chibois, is Christian Willer at La Palme d'Or, the restaurant of the Hôtel Martinez, where he is making a name for himself as an expert hand with fish.

At another hotel, the Juana in Juan-les-Pins, young Alain Ducasse—who at twenty-five had already spent six years with Guérard, Vergé, and Chapel—draws a large and enthusiastic crowd of diners at the restaurant La Terrasse. His chive-scented crayfish soup, his lobster and scallop ragoût, the fennel-steamed fish, and fantastic desserts will soon make anyone forget the smells of pizza and french fries that pervade Cannes.

Finally, there is a newcomer, previously

Every region of France is represented among the cheeses of this fromagerie in Cannes.

encountered in Alsace, who is emerging as a force to be reckoned with in Monte Carlo, where for years the worst and most expensive cuisine on the coast held sway. His name is Dominique Le Stanc, and his restaurant (of the same name) boasts a most original decor, featuring a collection of extraordinary toys. His modern, delicate cuisine has brought gracious dining back to Monaco, but watch out for the tab!

About two hundred fifty miles to the west, in the department of Aveyron, the prices look like relics from a bygone century. True, it is not easy to climb all the way up to Laguiole, a village in the Monts de l'Aubrac more popular with sheep than with tourists, where Michel Bras has his restaurant. Young Bras has never strayed from his rough stone house and the unspoiled country he holds so dear. Thus, his cooking shows no sign of outside influence; his style is wholly his own. The food he serves is simply astonishing and wonderfully delicious. Michel is a born artist. He designed the furniture of the small, rather modest hotel done in very good taste where he lives with his wife, his father (a former black-smith), and his mother, who, for her part, prepares the regional specialties favored chiefly by the local clientele of Lou Mazuc, as the restaurant is called in the dialect of Auvergne (it means "the house").

As for Michel, he goes off into the mountains to gather herbs and other plants or mushrooms or even flowers that he will use as he cooks, as his inspiration leads him; he is a fanatic for vegetables. Everything is extraordinary in this magical setting: the artichoke and fava bean bouillon seasoned with duck fat; the tiny leeks bathed in a vinaigrette scented with broom flowers; roast rabbit with milk "skin" and truffles; the sauté of crayfish and lamb with orange peel and corn; his crusty salmon with preserved onions; the celery and myrrh sherbets; or the crunchy chocolate puff pastry with almond milk cream. For the latter alone Bras should be awarded a Nobel prize for pastry-making.

Barely sixty miles southwest is a part of France that enjoys the special favor of the gods. It is called Gascony. It is the land of d'Artagnan in *The Three Musketeers*, of good living, of

Sheep in Berry, near Chateauroux, in the center of France.

abundance, and which, with its gentle hills and its gardens planted with peach, plum, and apricot trees, is one of the richest orchard lands in France. Not far from Agen, the prune capital of the world, in the village of Puymirol, Michel and Maryse Trama have restored an admirable dwelling which, in the thirteenth century, was a country seat belonging to the powerful counts of Toulouse. It took a lot of nerve and determination to launch such a project: who had ever heard of Puymirol? But the word gradually got around that L'Aubergade was one of the most engaging country inns of the southwest.

Inside is a splendid wooden staircase dating from the sixteenth century, huge beams, antique furniture, paintings, and pink-clothed tables in the dining room, each adorned with bouquets of wild flowers. It would be nice to spend the night at l'Aubergade, but, as yet, rooms are only in the planning stages. For the time being, you must content yourselves with Michel Trama's culinary talents. After a series of stints in small, ordinary Paris restaurants, he shows here that his own gift is anything but ordinary: from the fresh duck liver to the chocolate millefeuille, the truffled leek terrine, the roast capon with walnuts or the gingered veal, he shows himself to be a highly inventive chef.

Toulouse, the "pink city," is not far off, and, among the multitude of good reasons to stop there (Renaissance houses, museums, the special southern light and gaiety), one of them is a restaurant named Vanel. Lucien Vanel is a youthful man of fifty-odd years. He used to run a most traditional inn in the Quercy area; when he settled in Toulouse some time back, his cooking style underwent a startling metamorphosis. Drawing inspiration from regional recipes, he dreamed up all sorts of surprising and toothsome dishes. Located on the ground floor of a

Andre and Arnaud Daguin
Hôtel de France

modern building, the restaurant's decor is nothing to get excited about, but the lettuce stuffed with oysters, the prunes with bacon, the rabbit liver and scrambled egg tart, the crêpes stuffed with cèpe mushrooms, the frog soufflé, the cock and pig's trotters stewed in Cahors wine, and the millefeuille of caramelized pears cooked up by this graying chap in his culinary second youth are guaranteed to distract you from the uninspiring surroundings.

Over in Auch, in Armagnac country, a friend of Vanel's named André Daguin is one of the leading figures of Gascon gastronomy. A blustery former rugby player, Daguin is heart and soul attached to his native province, Gers, famed for its Armagnac, its foie gras, and its zest for life. As he neared forty, this dyed-in-the-wool traditionalist who had taken over the family establishment—the very bourgeois Hôtel de France—was seized by the urge to experiment and invent. He concocted an anthology of foie gras recipes (with puréed preserved garlic, with prawns, with sorrel purée, with blackberries) then published a cookbook entitled *The New Gascon Cookery*. And he ceaselessly adds unusual dishes to his menu, like oysters with smoked duck breast or his truffle sherbet.

Le Saint-James perches on a hilltop overlooking Bordeaux.

Saint-Jean-Pied-de-Port is a small but ancient fortified town near the Spanish border, with the grandiose Pyrénées as a backdrop. There, young Firmin Arrambide, who has taken charge of the old family hotel, called Les Pyrénées, is one of the best chefs of the new generation. Though the premises are not imposing, people come from far off to sample his hot mushroom pâté made with cèpes and girolles; peppers stuffed with salt cod and wrapped in an ultra-thin crêpe; bass broiled in its skin served with cooked-down tomatoes herbed with coriander and thyme; vegetable-stuffed rabbit; and his fruit terrine with almond mousse, capped off with a local pear brandy that may well be the world's best.

Before we close our tour of the southwest, we must make a halt in Bordeaux. Ten years back, the capital of Aquitaine could not boast a single great restaurant. That all changed with the arrival of a young chef named Jean-Marie Amat who virtually reinvented Bordeaux' regional cuisine, giving local gastronomy a tremendous boost. He is now established in an elegant restaurant, the Saint-James, perched on a green hilltop overlooking Bordeaux. Owners of large winegrowing estates and a hefty proportion of foreigners patronize this table, feasting on ravi-

oli stuffed with cèpe mushrooms, filets of eel sautéed with onions, the admirable duck liver, the broiled squab with Chinese spices, unforgettable desserts, and a wide selection of fascinating, little-known Bordeaux wines.

Amat's success spurred other young chefs to settle in Bordeaux, and three of their number have in their turn won celebrity status. Christian Clément, former assistant to Alain Senderens, after several years in a bistro in the old city, resettled at the well known Dubern, a restaurant whose decline had long saddened the citizens of Bordeaux. Then there is Jean Ramet, erstwhile pupil of Michel Guérard, who has opened the city's prettiest modern restaurant of the same name. And finally, Francis Garcia's restaurant, Clavel, where gratin of oysters with foie gras and duckling in Bordeaux testify that a Spaniard can be a great French chef.

The northwest peninsula of Brittany is a traditionalist province, poor in gastronomic resources other than what comes from the sea. Until quite recently, it had not a single great table; but now it too has been roused from its culinary torpor. To mention only the greatest chefs, we should cite Jean-Claude Gaudin, formerly a Guérard student, at the magnificent Château de Locguénolé in Hennebont near Lorient; Georges Paineau at Le Bretagne in Questembert (his resolutely contemporary cuisine is the most exciting in Brittany); and Olivier Roellinger at the Restaurant de Bricourt in Cancale, who forsook his career in chemical engineering to give himself over to his passion (and talent!) for cuisine.

Moving slightly west we arrive in the vast region called the Loire country, celebrated for its châteaux, its wines, its orchards, and its gentle pace of life. In Châteauroux is Jean Bardet, in his restaurant of the same name, who instant-

Jean Bardet

Didier Clément
Le Lion d'Or

ly wins one over with his hearty farmer's air, beneath which lurk great subtlety and wit. The same goes for his wife, Sophie, who is an expert in the art of matching food and wine. The food they serve reflects the couple's personality: attached to the land, yet overflowing with an almost staggering imagination, individuality, and inventiveness. It is hard to believe that Bardet spent a good part of his life in modest bistros, serving up steaks and fries, especially when you taste the exceptional oven-baked lobster served with duck gizzards in a sauce of Graves wine; his calf's head pot-au-feu; the carp steak marinated in olive oil and caramelized in Valençay wine; or the very simple leg of rabbit with a sauce made of Château-Chalon, served with crisp wild mushrooms and stewed artichokes, a memorable dish.

Each of Bardet's creations reveals original flavors, and that is the sign of a very great cook: someone who by juxtaposing basic tastes can create surprising new sensations. Even at this writing he may already have moved to Tours, where he has acquired an exquisite Napoleon III mansion set in a park, which will undoubtedly soon rank among the most attractive hotel-restaurants in France. Whether in Tours or in Chât-

eauroux, Bardet's restaurant merits a visit.

Between the châteaux of Blois and Chambord, another cook has been giving off sparks for a while now. His name is Bernard Robin, owner of Le Relais in Bracieux. He uses incomparably fresh raw materials (his father grows potatoes as flavorful as truffles). His table is accented by the subtle fragrances of fresh herbs, flawless flavor harmonies, and tasty Loire Valley wines. Try the spiced fresh cod, the rabbit in aspic with garden vegetables, the mixed grill of fish with potatoes in celery juice, the duck with a sauce that features essence of parsley, and squab with lemon sauce.

In Romorantin, in the heart of the impressive Sologne forest (a prime hunting region), is Le Lion d'Or, a cozy, comfortable country inn, where young Didier Clément prepares a remarkably delicate and original cuisine. All his dishes are artfully prepared and presented: the smoked salmon surrounding a slice of fresh salmon, lightly cooked and served with pink radishes in a creamy sauce; the frogs' legs with a purslane salad sparked with chives; the extraordinary roast prawns seasoned with a mixture of ten spices; the sweetbreads braised with grapefruit; the goat cheeses and the desserts. Didier's wife,

Christine, by the way, is an expert on the history of gastronomy. She is writing a voluminous thesis on the subject at the Sorbonne.

North, in Reims, Gerard Boyer is lord of the manor in the most sumptuous château-hotel France has seen for many a year. On fifteen acres of green lawns and gardens set in the heart of the city, the Château des Crayères was built in the nineteenth century for the owner of Pommery, the well-known Champagne label; it is luxurious, elegant, and most inviting. Gérard Boyer has prudently progressed from a classic culinary style to one that is not wholly modern, but that is personal and finely executed just the same. You could begin your meal with asparagus in puff pastry with oyster sauce, then go on to a splendid fricassée of lobster with morels or a broiled turbot garnished with a delicate, original sauce of red wine and acacia honey. Then there is the best veal kidney I've ever had the pleasure to eat, with leeks, mushrooms, and scallions; bring the meal to a close with a selection from the loaded dessert table, and don't forget to order Champagne. The wine list offers no fewer than 118 different Champagnes! And they are less costly here than just about anywhere else.

Lille is not far away, on the road to Belgium. Robert Bardot presides at Le Flambard, the most interesting restaurant in town, as well as one of the best tables in the Nord region, located in a house that dates from the reign of Louis XIV. This ultraclassically trained cook managed to break free from his bent for complicated dishes swimming in rich sauces. His cooking has a new simplicity and robustness, yet is as technically accomplished as ever. Notable proofs of this are the warm lobster salad with tarragon, pink-roasted pigeon served with a spice-stuffed peach—an exceptionally subtle dish—and admirable ravioli stuffed with foie gras and truffles. The wine cellar, stocked with Burgundies and Bordeaux, is sensational.

Our food lovers' pilgrimage comes to a close in Alsace, in Strasbourg, a bewitchingly beautiful city. Here love of a fine table isn't a sin, it's a virtue. The capital's top chef is Emile Jüng. He has progressed from a timid and conservative cook and has slowly but surely evolved (in Alsace, change does not happen quickly) a modern style. In a town where it was hard to find anything but sauerkraut on restaurant menus, Jüng has set a new tone for local Alsatian cuisine. In the airy and beautiful dining room of Le Crocodile, he serves a stunning goose and barley soup; a river perch in juniper-flavored cream; a singularly tender and flavorful cockerel in a Riesling sauce; duckling with juniper and ginger (a daring but perfectly successful match); or, during hunting season, a succulent pheasant with lentils and thyme. Like Haeberlin in Illhaeusern, Emile Jüng reveres the wines of his native Alsace.

Château des Crayères, in Reims, offers one hundred varieties of Champagne on its menu.

Alain Senderens
Lucas-Carton

EMINCE DE CHEVREUIL AU BEURRE DE GENIEVRE ET BAIES ROSES

ROAST VENISON WITH JUNIPER BUTTER SAUCE

MARINADE:

1	bottle hearty red wine
10	shallots, thinly sliced
¼	cup raspberry vinegar
¼	cup fresh lime juice
1	large bunch parsley stems
2¼	pounds venison fillet, barded and tied

GARNISHES:

3	small celery roots (about ⅔ pound each), peeled
	About 3 cups milk
	Salt and freshly ground pepper
¾	pound pâte brisée
1	fennel bulb, trimmed, cored, and finely diced
2	ribs celery, peeled and finely diced
3	cups heavy cream
1	red bell pepper, cored and finely diced
1	green bell pepper, cored and finely diced
2	large bunches parsley, all stems removed (about 6½ cups leaves)

VEGETABLE MIXTURE:

1	large green bell pepper, cored and cut into ¾-inch squares
1	large red bell pepper, cored and cut into ¾-inch squares
1	large leek, washed and cut into ¾-inch squares
½	head green cabbage, cored, large leaves de-ribbed
	Dried zest of 1 clementine, cut into thin julienne
3	tablespoons unsalted butter
2	teaspoons drained pink peppercorns
	Salt and freshly ground pepper

SAUCE:

1¼	cups unsalted butter blended with 80 coarsely ground juniper berries

Prepare marinade: In a large noncorrodible casserole, combine wine, shallots, vinegar, lime juice, and parsley. Add venison and marinate at cool room temperature, turning occasionally, for 4 hours.

Prepare garnishes: Halve celery roots crosswise and cut a small slice from the bottom of each so they sit flat. Rinse well. With a melon baller, carefully scoop out inside of each half, leaving a ½-inch shell. Place celery roots in a medium saucepan and add enough milk to cover. Season with salt and pepper and bring to a boil. Simmer over medium heat for about 30 minutes or until celery root "cups" are tender. Drain, rinse, and set aside.

Preheat oven to 400 degrees.

Roll out pastry to ⅛-inch thick. With a 5-inch round or fluted cookie cutter, stamp out 12 circles (you may have to reroll the dough). Line 12 3-inch round or fluted tartlet pans with pastry circles. Line each mold with aluminum foil, fill with dried beans, and place in the freezer for about 10 minutes. Arrange tartlet pans on a cookie sheet and bake for 10 minutes. Remove foil and beans and continue baking for about 10 minutes or until pastry is fully cooked and golden brown. Unmold tartlet shells onto a rack to cool.

In a saucepan of boiling salted water, blanch the fennel and celery together for 2 minutes. Drain well and place in a small saucepan with ½ cup heavy cream.

In another saucepan of boiling salted water, blanch red and green peppers for 2 minutes. Drain well and place in a small saucepan with ½ cup heavy cream.

Cook parsley leaves in a steamer for 6 minutes. Remove from steamer and when cool enough to handle, squeeze out as much liquid as possible. Place in a small saucepan with ¾ cup heavy cream.

Set all 3 saucepans over medium heat and cook each mixture for about 20 minutes or until cream reduces and thickens and vegetables are tender. Season with salt and pepper to taste.

Place celery roots, hollowed side up, in a baking dish just large enough to hold them and fill with fennel-celery mixture. Pour remaining heavy cream into baking dish and braise in the oven for 15 minutes.

Prepare vegetable mixture: In a large saucepan of boiling salted water, blanch green and red pepper, leek, cabbage, and clementine zests for 4 minutes. Drain well. In a large skillet, melt butter. Add blanched vegetables and cook over medium heat, stirring occasionally, for about 15 minutes or until tender. Stir in pink peppercorns and season with salt and pepper.

Prepare venison and sauce: Remove venison from casserole and dry well with paper towels. Set casserole over medium-high heat and boil marinade for about 40 minutes or until reduced to ½ cup. Strain through a fine-mesh strainer set over a medium saucepan.

Season venison with salt and pepper and roast it in the oven for 30 minutes (it will be quite rare). Transfer to a cutting board, cover with aluminum foil, and let rest in a warm place for 15 minutes.

Bring strained marinade to a boil over high heat and cook for about 5 minutes or until reduced to ¼ cup. Reduce heat to medium low and whisk in juniper butter, a few tablespoons at a time; strain and season with salt and pepper.

To serve: Reheat tartlet shells and celery roots in the oven. Reheat vegetable mixture, peppers in cream, and creamed parsley. Fill 6 tartlet shells with peppers, and 6 with parsley mixture. Drain stuffed celery roots. Slice venison and place on 6 large heated plates. Garnish each serving with a stuffed celery root, one of each tartlet, and a large spoonful of vegetable mixture. Carefully reheat sauce, if necessary, and spoon onto plates or pass separately in a sauceboat.

Makes 6 servings

Joël Robuchon

MIGNONNETTES DE CHEVREUIL POELEES A L'AIGRE-DOUX

SWEET AND SOUR VENISON MIGNONNETTES

1½	ounces fresh truffle, minced
6	tablespoons chopped parsley
1½	pounds venison fillet, trimmed and cut into 12 slices, plus 1 ounce venison, minced
2	large egg yolks, lightly beaten
½	cup unsalted butter
1	tablespoon shallots, minced
⅔	ounce black chanterelles, rinsed, dried, and minced, or substitute other thin, membranous wild mushroom
½	cup flat leaf parsley, stems removed
1	ounce foie gras
1	ounce ground lean pork
2	ounces fresh ravioli dough
3	slices fresh pineapple, cut ¾-inch thick
	Salt and freshly ground pepper
1	tablespoon safflower oil
2	tablespoons aged wine vinegar
3	juniper berries
½	cup game or chicken stock
1	cup cooked cranberries

In a small bowl, combine 1 ounce minced truffle and chopped parsley. Dip each slice of venison in egg yolks, then coat with parsley-truffle mixture. Reserve.

In a small, heavy saucepan, melt 1 tablespoon butter. Add shallots and cook until soft, but not browned. Remove and reserve in a small bowl. Repeat procedure with wild mushrooms; remove from heat and combine with shallots. Blanch parsley in 1 cup boiling, salted water for 1 minute; drain and chop finely. Add to mushroom-shallot mixture along with foie gras, remaining minced truffle, minced venison, and pork. Combine well.

On a floured work surface, roll out ravioli dough as thin as possible and shape into 2 equal rectangles. With a small spoon, spoon mushroom mixture at 12 even intervals on one of the rectangles. With a brush dipped in water, moisten dough around each spoonful of filling and cover with second dough rectangle. Press pastry together between each ravioli and cut with a round cookie cutter.

Cut pineapple slices into quarters to give 12 small sections. In a heavy skillet, melt 2 tablespoons butter. Add pineapple and sauté for about 1 minute; remove from heat and cover.

Bring 1½ quarts water to a boil with ¼ teaspoon salt. Add ravioli and poach for 5 to 8 minutes; drain. In a small, heavy saucepan, heat 2 tablespoons butter, add ravioli and keep warm.

Season venison with salt and pepper to taste. In a large, heavy skillet, melt oil and 2 tablespoons butter. Add venison and sauté for about 3 minutes on each side; the meat should be pink. Transfer to a heated dish and keep warm. Degrease skillet and deglaze with 1 to 2 tablespoons wine vinegar. Add juniper berries and stock. Season to taste. Reheat cranberries.

To serve: Strain sauce and spoon a little onto each of 4 heated plates. Arrange 3 alternate slices of venison and pineapple on each plate. Place a spoonful of cranberries on each pineapple slice and arrange ravioli in center of plate. Serve immediately.

Makes 4 servings

Joël Robuchon alternates venison and pineapple to achieve a sweet-and-sour taste.

Joël Robuchon

SALADE DE HOMARD EN BOLERO

LOBSTER SALAD WITH TOMATO, APPLE, AND AVOCADO

3	quarts water
1	large carrot, sliced
1	large onion, sliced
1	rib celery, sliced
1	large bouquet garni
½	cup wine vinegar or 1¼ cups white wine
15	whole peppercorns
1	teaspoon salt
4	1-pound lobsters
⅓	cup wine vinegar
½	cup peanut oil
1½	tablespoons crème fraîche
	Salt and freshly ground pepper
2	large, ripe tomatoes, peeled
1	Golden Delicious apple, peeled
1	large, ripe avocado (preferably Haas), peeled
3	tablespoons fresh lemon juice
1	tablespoon sunflower oil
4	teaspoons snipped fresh chives
4	teaspoons fresh chervil leaves

100

In a large, non-aluminum stockpot, combine water, carrot, onion, celery, bouquet garni, vinegar, peppercorns, and salt. Bring to a boil over high heat, then reduce heat to medium and simmer for 30 minutes. Strain court bouillon into another large stockpot.

Return liquid to a boil over high heat. Add lobsters, head first. Reduce heat to medium and cook lobsters for 6 minutes. Remove from heat and let lobsters cool in the cooking liquid.

While lobsters cool, prepare salad. Pour vinegar into a small bowl and whisk in peanut oil, a little at a time. When all oil has been incorporated, whisk in crème fraîche. Season to taste with salt and pepper.

Halve tomatoes and carefully seed them without tearing the flesh. Using a tiny melon baller, carve out small rounds of tomato flesh. (If you don't have a melon baller, cut tomatoes into ¼-inch dice.) Place in a medium bowl.

Cut the apple and avocado in the same fashion (either in tiny balls or ¼-inch dice). In a small bowl, toss the apple and avocado with lemon juice to coat thoroughly; drain well and add to tomatoes. Cover and refrigerate.

When lobsters are cool enough to handle, remove them from their cooking liquid and dry well with paper towels. Separate the tails, forelegs, and claws from the bodies. Crack claws and try to remove meat in one piece. Remove tail and leg meat from shells. Place all lobster meat on a plate, cover and refrigerate until well-chilled. Reserve carcasses and empty shells for another use.

Pour about 3 tablespoons of vinaigrette onto each plate. Toss chilled lobster meat with remaining vinaigrette; drain lightly. Slice lobster tails into medallions ⅓-inch thick; remove any dark parts of intestine. Arrange medallions in a circle in the center of each plate. Place claws at the top of the plate and leg meat in the center of the medallions.

Toss tomato, apple, and avocado salad with sunflower oil and sprinkle a large soupspoonful over each serving. Garnish each plate with 1 teaspoon chives and 1 teaspoon chervil.

Makes 4 servings

Robuchon's cold lobster salad includes tomato, apple, and avocado.

Guy Savoy

OURSINS AUX CROSNES
SEA URCHINS WITH ARTICHOKES

4	large artichokes, stems and dark outer leaves removed
	Freshly squeezed lemon juice plus 1 lemon, halved
3	tablespoons flour
8	large or 12 small sea urchins
4	to 5 tablespoons cold unsalted butter
	Freshly ground pepper

Remove all leaves from artichokes, cutting them about 1½ inches from base, level with choke; rub cut surfaces with lemon juice to prevent discoloration. Beginning at stem ends, use a sharp knife to cut around base and sides, trimming away all traces of dark green leaves. With knife held at an angle, trim tops around chokes; rub cut surfaces with lemon juice as you go.

Place trimmed artichoke bottoms in a medium, nonreactive saucepan and cover with cold water. Whisk in flour. Squeeze juice from lemon halves and add juice and lemon to pan. Bring to a boil over high heat. Reduce heat to medium and simmer for about 20 minutes or until artichokes are just tender when pierced with a knife. Let artichokes cool in cooking liquid.

Meanwhile, prepare sea urchins. Hold one urchin in a towel, with its mouth facing you. Insert the tip of pointy kitchen scissors into mouth. Cut out a large circle around mouth, grasp underside with scissors, and lift it out. Invert urchin over a fine-mesh sieve, set over a small saucepan, and gently shake out juices. With a small spoon, scoop out orange roe, which clings to inside of urchin shell in a star pattern, and place in a bowl. Repeat with remaining urchins.

Gently rinse roe in cold water and drain on paper towels. Add roe to strained urchin juices in saucepan.

Remove artichokes from cooking liquid and drain on paper towels. With a small spoon, scoop out hairy chokes. Thinly slice artichoke bottoms and divide among 4 serving plates, fanning the slices decoratively.

Warm urchin roe over low heat. Carefully remove roe with a slotted spoon and divide among plates.

Bring urchin liquid to a boil over high heat. Remove from heat and whisk in butter, 2 tablespoons at a time. Season sauce with pepper and lemon juice to taste and spoon it over artichokes and urchin roe. Serve immediately.

Makes 4 servings

Ed. note: The original version of this recipe calls for crosnes, *a small root vegetable not available in this country. The chef suggests using artichoke bottoms in their place. Sea urchin roe is available at Japanese fish markets.*

Guy Savoy combines sea urchins and a vegetable in this unusual dish.

Guy Savoy

SOUPE A L'EMINCE DE POISSON
SLICED FISH SOUP WITH SAFFRON

1	pound fish bones, preferably a mixture of sole and sea eel, well-rinsed
1	onion, sliced
8	parsley stems
2	quarts cold water
3	tablespoons olive oil
1	carrot, finely diced
1	onion, finely chopped
1	leek, white and tender green, well-washed and finely chopped
1	ripe tomato, peeled, seeded, and chopped
1	bouquet garni
1	clove garlic, finely chopped
	Pinch of saffron threads
3	tablespoons heavy cream
	Pinch of thyme
	Salt and freshly ground pepper
³⁄₄	pound fish fillets: 1 small piece monkfish, thinly sliced; 1 small piece red snapper, unskinned, cut into pieces; 1 small piece sole or whiting, cut into ¹⁄₃-inch strips
	Fresh chervil leaves

In a large stockpot, combine fish bones, onion, parsley stems, and water; bring to a boil over medium-high heat. Reduce heat to medium and simmer stock, skimming frequently, for 15 minutes. Strain stock through a very fine mesh strainer.

In a large casserole, heat olive oil. Add the carrot, onion, and leek and cook over medium heat, stirring occasionally, for about 10 minutes or until vegetables are soft. Add tomato and cook 1 minute longer. Stir in fish stock, bouquet garni, and garlic; bring to a boil over high heat. With a ladle, skim surface of soup until it is clear of foam. Add saffron and simmer soup over medium heat for 40 minutes.

Meanwhile, preheat oven to 375 degrees.

Place 4 large ovenproof soup plates or bowls on a baking sheet and heat in the oven until very hot.

Stir cream and thyme into soup and season with salt and pepper to taste. Ladle 1 cup soup into each bowl and evenly distribute sliced fish among bowls. Bake in preheated oven for exactly 2 minutes. Fill bowls with remaining soup, sprinkle with chervil leaves, and serve immediately.   Makes 4 servings

Facing page: Guy Savoy's fish-and-saffron soup.

Right: Alain Dutournier bakes hen pheasants in a flower-shaped tart.

Alain Dutournier

CROUSTADE DE POULE FAISAN AUX CHAMPIGNONS SAUVAGES
HEN PHEASANTS WITH WILD MUSHROOMS

2	hen pheasants, boned, with bones chopped and reserved
1	teaspoon Dijon-style mustard
¹⁄₄	teaspoon juniper berries, ground
¹⁄₄	teaspoon ground nutmeg
1	clove, ground
4	tablespoons port wine
1¹⁄₄	cups white wine
	Salt and freshly ground pepper
¹⁄₂	cup unsalted butter, plus 4 tablespoons unsalted butter, melted
2	carrots, peeled and chopped
5	shallots, chopped, plus 1 tablespoon chopped shallot
1¹⁄₂	ounces dried cèpes, soaked in water and drained, plus ³⁄₄ pound fresh cèpes
1	cup crème fraîche
3	tablespoons parsley, chopped
³⁄₄	pound fresh girolles
³⁄₄	pound fresh pieds de mouton
5	to 8, 8-by-16-inch sheets phyllo or thin strudel dough

(Recipe continued on following page.)

105

Cut pheasants into small pieces. In a large bowl, combine mustard, juniper berries, nutmeg, clove, 2 tablespoons port, ¼ cup white wine, and salt and pepper to taste; mix well. Baste pheasant pieces with mixture and marinate overnight in the refrigerator.

Preheat oven to 350 degrees. In a large, heavy saucepan, melt 2 tablespoons butter. Add carrots, 5 chopped shallots, and reserved bones and sauté for about 5 minutes or until vegetables are golden in color. Deglaze with remaining port and white wine. Simmer to reduce; strain and add soaked cèpes and crème fraîche. Transfer to a blender and process until smooth; keep warm in a double boiler.

In a heavy skillet, melt 6 tablespoons butter. Add remaining 1 tablespoon chopped shallot, parsley, fresh cèpes, and salt and pepper to taste. Sauté for 5 to 8 minutes or until moisture is released and mushrooms soften. Remove from heat and let cool.

Brush pastry sheets with melted butter and place in buttered tart pan with removable bottom; pastry should overlap at least 3 inches on all sides of pan. Remove pheasant from marinade and drain. Fill tart with pheasant and cooled mushrooms. Fold pastry over filling and arrange in a flower design in center of tart. Bake in preheated oven for 40 minutes. Serve with warm sauce.

Makes 4 to 6 servings

106

A piperade of onions, tomatoes and bell peppers surrounds Dutournier's salmon fillet.

Alain Dutournier

SAUMON AU LARD ET LA PIPERADE

SALMON FILLET WITH PANCETTA, BASIL, AND A PIPERADE

6½	ounces pancetta or meaty salt pork, cut into 12 thin slices
2¼	pounds unskinned salmon fillets (center cut), cut into 6 equal pieces
	Salt and freshly ground pepper
24	fresh basil leaves
7	ounces pork caul, soaked, drained, and cut into 6 large rectangles
1	tablespoon vegetable oil
12	small white onions (about 1 pound), thinly sliced
¼	pound prosciutto, fat and lean, cut into julienne
3	cloves garlic, crushed
2	green bell peppers, cored, deribbed, and cut into julienne
3	ripe tomatoes, peeled, seeded, and chopped

In a medium saucepan, cover pancetta slices with cold water. Bring to a boil and simmer for 10 minutes. Drain, rinse, and set aside on paper towels.

Cut a horizontal pocket in each piece of salmon and season inside and out with salt and pepper. Stuff each pocket with 1 slice pancetta and 2 basil leaves. Top each piece of salmon with another slice pancetta and 2 more basil leaves. Wrap each prepared salmon fillet in a caul rectangle and place, skin side down, in a paper-towel-lined baking dish; refrigerate.

Preheat oven to 450 degrees.

In a large skillet, heat oil. Add onions and prosciutto and sauté over medium-high heat, stirring frequently for about 10 minutes or until golden. Add garlic and bell peppers and sauté for about 5 minutes until peppers soften. Add tomatoes, cover, and cook over medium-low heat, stirring occasionally, for about 10 minutes or until vegetables are very tender and tomatoes have cooked down.

Bake salmon in preheated oven for about 10 minutes or until a skewer inserted into the center is very warm to the touch.

Meanwhile, reheat piperade and season to taste with salt and pepper. Serve salmon on very hot plates, surrounded with piperade.

Makes 6 servings

Dominique Nahmias

TURBOT AUX CITRONS CONFITS ET AU FENOUIL

TURBOT WITH PRESERVED LEMONS AND FENNEL

2	large fennel bulbs, cored and thinly sliced
1	large rib celery, cut into julienne
1/3	cup olive oil
1	teaspoon paprika
	Pinch of cayenne pepper
1	large tomato, peeled, seeded, and diced
4	black olives, pitted and diced
1/3	preserved lemon, diced
3	tablespoons coarsely chopped parsley
4	7-ounce turbot fillets
	Salt and freshly ground pepper
1/3	cup fish stock
1/3	cup dry white wine
8	coriander seeds, crushed
1/2	teaspoon cumin seeds
1/2	teaspoon coarsely cracked black pepper
8	sprigs fresh cilantro

Preheat oven to 400 degrees.

Blanch fennel in boiling, salted water for 1 minute. Add celery and blanch for 1 minute longer. Drain vegetables, refresh under cold water, and drain again.

In a small bowl, combine olive oil, paprika, and cayenne pepper. Coat bottom of a large nonreactive baking dish with 3½ tablespoons seasoned olive oil. Add fennel, celery, tomato, olives, preserved lemon, and parsley and toss to coat.

Season turbot fillets with salt and pepper and place them in baking dish, on top of vegetables. With a pastry brush, paint fillets with remaining 1½ tablespoons seasoned oil. Sprinkle stock and white wine over fish. Bake in preheated oven for about 17 minutes or until fish is firm and just flakes when pierced with a knife.

To serve: Place a turbot fillet on each of 4 plates and surround with vegetables. Sprinkle each fillet with crushed coriander, cumin seeds, and black pepper. Garnish each serving with 2 sprigs cilantro and serve immediately.

Makes 4 servings

The preserved lemons used in this dish are available at Middle Eastern groceries.

Michel Rostang

LE DOS D'AGNEAU ROTI A L'OS, AUX ECHALOTES MARINEES A L'HUILE D'OLIVE VIERGE ET VIEUX VINAIGRE DE VIN, FLAN DE COURGETTES

ROAST RACK OF LAMB WITH SHALLOTS AND A ZUCCHINI FLAN

ZUCCHINI FLAN:
- 2 tablespoons butter
- 1 teaspoon salt
- 2 pounds young zucchini, peeled, with some green remaining
- ½ cup virgin olive oil
- ½ cup fresh white breadcrumbs, soaked in ½ cup milk
- 2 ounces Gruyère cheese, diced
- 4 eggs

RACK OF LAMB:
- 1 whole rack of lamb (7 to 8 pounds), split, chined, trimmed, frenched, and cut into 6 pieces of 3 chops each
- ¼ cup virgin olive oil
- 2 dozen shallots, peeled and finely chopped, plus 6 shallots, unpeeled and steamed
  Aged wine vinegar to taste

108

Prepare zucchini flan: Preheat oven to 350 degrees. Butter 12 2¼-by-2⅓-inch dariole molds. In a large pot, bring 3 to 4 quarts water to a boil. Add salt and zucchini. Cook, uncovered, for 6 to 8 minutes. Transfer zucchini to a bowl of ice water to cool; drain and cut into small pieces.

In a food processor fitted with a metal blade, combine zucchini, olive oil, breadcrumbs, milk, cheese, and eggs. Process until mixture is smooth and zucchini is finely shredded. Pour mixture into prepared molds and arrange in an ovenproof or metal pan. Fill pan with enough water to come about halfway up sides of molds. Bake in preheated oven for 20 to 25 minutes or until set. Remove from oven and keep warm.

Prepare lamb: Increase oven temperature to 400 degrees. In a heavy saucepan, heat oil over low heat. Add chopped shallots and cook, stirring with a wooden spoon, for 5 to 8 minutes or until golden. Remove from heat and set aside.

In a heavy skillet, brown lamb over high heat for 5 to 8 minutes. Transfer to a large baking pan, add steamed shallots, and bake in preheated oven for 15 to 25 minutes. Remove from oven and let meat set for 5 minutes before carving; reserve juices.

To serve: Reheat chopped shallots; add any reserved lamb juices and vinegar to taste. With a sharp knife, carve lamb. (You can either divide each portion into 3 separate chops or bone the meat and slice thinly.) Arrange meat in center of 6 heated serving plates. Spoon chopped shallots at bottom of each plate and place a whole steamed shallot, peeled and halved, at top. With a sharp knife, loosen flans from molds and invert 2 onto each plate.

Makes 6 servings

Zucchini flan accompanies Michel Rostang's roast rack of lamb.

Dominique Nahmias

RAVIOLES DE HOMARDS
LOBSTER RAVIOLI

LOBSTER RAVIOLI:

2   1½-pound female lobsters (with eggs, if possible)

40   thin wonton skins

⅓   cup peeled, seeded, diced tomato

⅓   cup crème fraîche plus 1 cup crème fraîche, warmed

     Salt and freshly ground cayenne pepper

1   large egg yolk

30   fresh chervil leaves

LOBSTER BISQUE:

     Shells and carcasses from 2 lobsters

2   tablespoons olive oil

1   carrot, peeled and chopped

1   onion, peeled and chopped

1¼   cups white wine

1¼   cups water

2   tablespoons tomato paste

½   cup crème fraîche

2   tablespoons unsalted butter

110

Prepare lobster ravioli: Preheat oven to 425 degrees. Bake lobsters in preheated oven for 5 minutes. Separate tail and claws from lobsters and remove flesh from each, in one piece; reserve coral, eggs, shells, and carcasses.

Slice lobster tails as thin as possible. On a work surface, spread out 20 wonton skins and arrange about 1½ teaspoons sliced lobster on each. Combine tomato and crème fraîche and season with salt and cayenne pepper to taste. Spoon about 1 teaspoon tomato mixture, a few lobster eggs, and a chervil leaf on each prepared ravioli. With a brush dipped in egg yolk, paint remaining 20 wonton skins and cover prepared ravioli, pressing around filled portions to seal. With a 2½-inch cookie cutter, cut out ravioli.

Prepare lobster bisque: With a meat pounder or rolling pin, crush reserved lobster shells and carcasses. In a large, heavy saucepan, heat olive oil. Add crushed lobsters and sauté for a few minutes. Add carrot and onion and cook over medium heat until golden in color. Add wine, water, and tomato paste and bring to a boil. Simmer for 20 to 25 minutes, then strain through a fine-mesh sieve set over a saucepan. Return bisque to heat and reduce to about 1¼ cups. Reduce heat to low and whisk in crème fraîche; set aside.

To serve: Poach ravioli in boiling, lightly salted water for about 3 minutes. Remove from heat and drain; reserve poaching liquid and use it to reheat lobster claws. In a bowl, combine ravioli and warm crème fraîche; toss to coat evenly. Heat bisque and season with cayenne pepper and salt to taste. Over low heat, whisk in 2 tablespoons butter and lobster coral; do not boil.

Place 5 ravioli in each of 4 heated dishes and spoon a ribbon of bisque around them. Garnish with chervil leaves and a whole lobster claw.

Makes 4 servings

In an unusual combination, Dominique Nahmias serves lobster ravioli with lobster bisque.

ROSACE DE TOMATE FARCIE AUX CHAMPIGNONS, AUX NAVETS FONDANTS ET AUX ESCARGOTS BEURRE VERT PRE

SNAIL-AND-MUSHROOM-STUFFED TOMATO AND TURNIP ROSACE WITH GREEN HERB BUTTER

SNAIL-AND-MUSHROOM-STUFFED TOMATO:

5	firm, ripe medium tomatoes, peeled
¼	pound mushrooms, trimmed and finely chopped
½	lemon, juiced
2	tablespoons unsalted butter
1	tablespoon minced shallots
1	small clove garlic, minced
1	dozen snails, without shells, or substitute ¾ cup fish, shellfish, or meat
½	teaspoon Dijon-style mustard
	Salt and freshly ground pepper
⅔	cup crème fraîche
1	tablespoon finely chopped fresh chives
1	tablespoon olive oil

BEURRE VERT PRE:

1	small bunch parsley, stemmed and coarsely chopped
½	bunch watercress, thick stems removed and coarsely chopped
20	chives, coarsely chopped
15	shoots of chervil, coarsely chopped, plus 4 shoots, stems removed, optional
½	cup cold water
7	tablespoons cold unsalted butter, cut into small pieces
½	teaspoon red wine vinegar
	Salt and freshly ground pepper

FONDANT TURNIPS:

½	pound small white turnips, peeled and cut into 16 even pieces
1	tablespoon unsalted butter

Prepare snail-and-mushroom-stuffed tomato: Preheat oven to 300 degrees. Cut 4 tomatoes into even quarters. Remove and discard interior, seeds, and juice. Lightly salt tomatoes and set aside. Remove seeds and juice from remaining tomato, then chop finely and reserve.

In a small saucepan, place mushrooms, lemon juice, and 1 tablespoon butter. Add enough water to partially cover mushrooms and cook, covered, over medium heat for about 8 minutes. Remove from heat and drain.

In a heavy saucepan, melt 1 tablespoon butter. Add shallots and garlic and cook until lightly colored. Add snails and 1 tablespoon reserved chopped tomato. Cook over low heat for about 3 minutes. Add mushrooms and stir well. Season with mustard and salt and pepper to taste. Cook over low heat, add crème fraîche, and simmer for 5 minutes. Remove from heat and add chives.

Prepare beurre vert pre: In a small saucepan, place parsley, watercress, chives, chopped chervil, and cold water. Bring to a slow boil and cook about 3 minutes. Remove from heat and set aside to cool. Drain, reserving liquid, and transfer herbs to a food processor or blender. Process until puréed and add a few teaspoons of reserved cooking liquid to smooth mixture. Transfer puréed herbs to a small, heavy saucepan and cook, whisking constantly, over low heat. Add butter, a few pieces at a time. Season with vinegar and salt and pepper to taste. Transfer sauce to blender and process for 1 to 2 seconds. Keep sauce warm or reheat at serving time.

Prepare fondant turnips: With a small paring knife, trim turnips to olive shapes. Cook in boiling salted water for about 3 minutes; strain and transfer to a bowl of ice water to cool.

Drain and set aside.

To serve: Preheat oven to 300 degrees. Drain excess liquid from quartered tomatoes and place them in an ovenproof dish with 1½ tablespoons reserved chopped tomatoes. Heat in preheated oven for about 3 minutes. Reheat snails.

In a heavy saucepan, melt 1 tablespoon butter. Add turnips and cook over medium heat for 4 to 5 minutes or until warmed, but not colored. Salt to taste. Reheat beurre vert pre and spoon it onto 4 warmed shallow plates. With 2 oval soupspoons, form warm snail mixture into 16 even ovals; place 4 ovals in a spoke pattern on each plate. Cover with warm tomato quarters, pointed ends facing rim of plate, and intersperse decoratively with fondant turnips. Dip a brush into olive oil and lightly paint each tomato petal. Place a teaspoon of reserved chopped tomato in center of each plate. Sprinkle with chervil, if desired. Serve immediately.

Makes 4 servings

In Georges Blanc's brilliantly colored dish, tomato quarters are stuffed with snails and mushrooms and arranged in herb butter.

LA SUITE DES TROIS DESSERTS AU CHOCOLAT ET A LA MENTHE FRAICHE

TRIO OF CHOCOLATE DESSERTS WITH FRESH MINT

ICE CREAM:

2	cups milk
3½	tablespoons honey
2	ounces semisweet chocolate, chopped
6	egg yolks
⅓	cup granulated sugar
¾	cup unsweetened cocoa powder

CREME ANGLAISE:

2	cups milk
1	vanilla bean, split
6	egg yolks
⅓	cup granulated sugar
¼	cup chopped fresh mint leaves

MOUSSE CAKE:

13	ounces semisweet chocolate, chopped
3	tablespoons heavy cream plus 1 cup heavy cream, beaten until stiff
2	eggs, separated
1	tablespoon plus 1 teaspoon granulated sugar

SOUFFLE:

	Butter and sugar, for the molds
2	eggs, separated, plus 2 egg whites
⅓	cup plus 1½ tablespoons granulated sugar
2	tablespoons unsweetened cocoa powder
	Fresh mint leaves

114

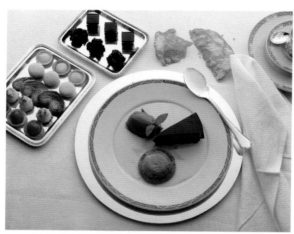

A trio of chocolate desserts from Michel and Jean-Michel Lorain.

Prepare ice cream: In a medium saucepan, bring milk and honey to a boil over medium-high heat. Remove from heat, add chopped chocolate, and stir until melted. In a bowl, whisk egg yolks with sugar until thoroughly blended; whisk in cocoa. Gradually whisk in hot milk mixture. Return to saucepan and cook over medium-low heat, whisking constantly for about 10 minutes or until thickened. Transfer to a large bowl and refrigerate until cold. Pour cooled mixture into an ice cream machine and freeze according to the manufacturer's directions.

Prepare crème anglaise: In a medium saucepan, scald milk with vanilla bean. In a bowl, whisk egg yolks with sugar. Gradually whisk hot milk into yolk mixture. Return mixture to saucepan and cook over medium-low heat, stirring constantly with a wooden spoon, for about 15 minutes or until custard thickens. Pour custard into a bowl, stir in mint, and refrigerate until cold.

Prepare mousse cake: In a double boiler, melt 7 ounces chocolate. Meanwhile, use a pencil to trace three 8-inch circles on a large sheet of parchment paper. When chocolate is melted and completely smooth, pour one third of it into center of each circle. With a spatula, spread chocolate into a thin, even layer, following traced patterns. Let cool at room temperature until set.

In a double boiler, heat remaining chocolate and 3 tablespoons cream, stirring occasionally, until chocolate is melted. Whisk in egg yolks and transfer mixture to a large bowl; cool to room temperature.

Meanwhile, in a large bowl, beat egg whites with sugar until stiff peaks form. When chocolate mixture is cool, fold in beaten whites. When whites are almost fully incorporated, fold in whipped heavy cream.

Carefully remove chocolate disks from parchment paper. Reserve most perfect disk for top of cake. Place a disk on a large plate and spoon half the mousse mixture onto it. With a spatula, spread mousse to edges. Cover with a second disk and spread with remaining mousse. Top with last disk and refrigerate until serving time.

Prepare soufflé: Preheat oven to 450 degrees. Butter six ⅔-cup ramekins and dust lightly with sugar; refrigerate.

In a small bowl, whisk egg yolks with 2½ tablespoons sugar until pale and fluffy; whisk in 1 tablespoon cocoa. In a large bowl, beat egg whites with remaining sugar until stiff peaks form. Fold in remaining cocoa. Stir a little of the whites into the egg yolk mixture to lighten, then fold yolk mixture into whites until well combined. Arrange prepared ramekins on a cookie sheet, fill with soufflé mixture, and bake on the bottom rack of the oven for about 12 minutes or until puffed and set.

To serve: Strain crème anglaise and pour it onto 6 large dessert plates. Heat a large slicing knife under hot water, wipe dry, and cut mousse cake into 6 slices. Place a slice of cake and a large scoop of ice cream on each plate. As soon as soufflés are ready, unmold them, turn right-side-up, and arrange on plates. Garnish each serving with fresh mint leaves and serve immediately.

Makes 6 servings

Ed. note: In this dessert assembly, three chocolate confections of different temperature and texture are served together.

Bernard Loiseau

LE RAGOUT DE LEGUMES AU CERFEUIL

VEGETABLE RAGOUT WITH CHERVIL

8	to 10 baby carrots
3	to 4 small white turnips, peeled
2	to 3 young zucchini
10	to 12 small white onions and/or green onions, trimmed
6	tablespoons unsalted butter
1½	cups green cabbage, thinly sliced, or broccoli florets
½	medium red pepper, cut into ⅓-inch dice
½	teaspoon olive oil
½	cup cold water
1	teaspoon fresh lemon juice
	Salt and freshly ground pepper
¼	cup fresh chervil leaves

With a small paring knife, slice the carrots, turnips, and zucchini into similar-size ovals. In each of 4 small saucepans, place carrots, onions, turnips, and zucchini and add enough water to barely cover vegetables. Add 1 tablespoon butter to each pan and cook over medium heat for 3 to 7 minutes. Blanch cabbage in boiling water for 1 minute. In a small skillet, sauté red pepper in olive oil over medium heat for about 1 minute.

In a large, heavy-bottomed saucepan, melt remaining 2 tablespoons butter. Add carrots, turnips, zucchini, and onions and sauté over medium heat for about 1 minute or until pale golden in color, but not browned. Deglaze with cold water and lemon juice. Add blanched cabbage, red pepper, and salt and pepper to taste. Serve in a deep dish garnished with chervil.

Makes 4 servings

115

Overleaf: The simplest of ingredients from the garden are transformed by Bernard Loiseau into a sophisticated vegetable ragoût.

ROMAN
VOSNE
J. Drouhin
Beaune
FRANÇAISE NON RECONSTITUÉE
Française non Reconstituée · Appellation Contrôlée
Duvault-Blochet
Chambon
Seuls propriétaires

Bernard Loiseau

LE FEUILLETE A L'ORANGE

GRAND MARNIER ICE CREAM IN PUFF PASTRY WITH ORANGES AND RASPBERRY SAUCE

ICE CREAM:

3	cups milk
²/₃	cup granulated sugar
1	vanilla bean, split lengthwise
12	egg yolks
1	teaspoon Grand Marnier

CANDIED ORANGE ZEST:

6	small navel oranges, well-washed
1¹/₃	cups sugar
1¹/₃	cups water
2	tablespoons grenadine

PASTRY AND SAUCE:

1	pound frozen puff pastry, defrosted
3	pints raspberries
	Powdered sugar
2	small navel oranges
2	tablespoons unsalted butter
2	tablespoons granulated sugar
	Fresh mint leaves

118

Prepare ice cream mixture: In a medium saucepan, combine milk with ¹/₃ cup sugar and the vanilla bean; bring to a boil over medium heat.

Meanwhile, in a medium bowl, whisk egg yolks with remaining ¹/₃ cup sugar until pale and thick. Whisk hot milk into egg yolk mixture until thoroughly blended, then return mixture to saucepan. Cook over medium heat, stirring constantly with a wooden spoon, for about 12 minutes or until mixture is thick enough to coat the back of the spoon. Remove from heat and strain into a bowl. Let cool slightly, then refrigerate until well-chilled.

Prepare candied orange zest: With a vegetable peeler or a sharp knife, strip zests from oranges and cut into fine julienne. Reserve oranges. In a medium, heavy-based saucepan, bring the sugar and water to a boil over medium-high heat. When the sugar has dissolved, add julienned zests and grenadine and cook over medium heat for about 15 minutes or until zests are lightly candied. With a wire skimmer or a fork, transfer zests to a lightly oiled wire rack to cool.

Preheat oven to 400 degrees.

With a sharp knife, finely chop candied zests. Add them to ice cream mixture and stir in Grand Marnier. Pour mixture into an ice cream machine and freeze according to the manufacturer's directions.

Prepare pastry and sauce: With a 4¹/₂-inch fluted cookie cutter, stamp out 8 rounds from the puff pastry. Set rounds on a heavy baking sheet and bake in preheated oven for about 12 minutes or until puffed and browned. Transfer to a rack to cool.

Purée raspberries in a food mill or a food processor. Strain purée into a bowl and sift in powdered sugar to taste. Refrigerate sauce.

With a sharp knife, peel the 2 oranges and the 6 that were stripped of zest; remove all bitter white pith. Slice in between membranes to remove sections. In a large skillet, melt butter over medium-low heat. Add orange sections and sugar and cook, tossing constantly, until warmed through, about 1 minute. Remove from heat.

Assemble dessert: Cut pastries in half horizontally. Sift powdered sugar over pastry tops. Spoon raspberry sauce onto 8 plates, place a pastry bottom on each; and surround with orange sections. Place a scoop of ice cream on each pastry and cover with sugared tops. Garnish each serving with mint leaves and serve immediately.

Makes 8 servings

Bernard Loiseau's Grand Marnier ice cream with raspberry sauce.

Jacques Chibois

LE PAPILLON DE LANGOUSTINES A LA CHIFFONADE DE MESCLUN

BUTTERFLY OF LANGOUSTINES WITH BASIL CHIFFONADE

BUTTERFLY OF LANGOUSTINES:

12	to 20 fresh langoustines or large shrimp, unshelled
	Salt and freshly ground pepper
1½	quarts water
½	pound green beans, trimmed
1	bunch arugula, mâche, watercress, or other salad greens
1	to 2 small zucchini, sliced into 1/16-by-2½-inch strips
8	whole fresh basil leaves, plus 8 fresh basil leaves, cut widthwise into thin strips for chiffonade
8	small cherry tomatoes

CITRUS VINAIGRETTE:

2	medium oranges, peeled, membrane removed, and divided into sections
1	lemon, peeled, membrane removed, and divided into sections
½	cup olive oil
10	fresh basil leaves, optional
¼	teaspoon ground coriander seeds
1	ripe tomato, peeled, seeded, and finely chopped
	Salt and freshly ground pepper

Prepare butterfly of langoustines: Steam langoustines for 8 to 10 minutes. From 4 langoustines, remove only tail shell; remove entire shell from remaining langoustines. Place all langoustines in an ovenproof dish and season with salt and pepper.

In a large enamel or stainless-steel pot, bring water to a boil. Add 1 teaspoon salt and green beans; blanch for 5 to 8 minutes or until tender-crisp. With a slotted spoon, transfer beans to a bowl of ice water to cool; drain immediately.

Prepare citrus vinaigrette: In a blender, combine orange and lemon sections, olive oil, basil, and coriander. Blend to emulsify. In a small saucepan, combine orange mixture, chopped tomato, and salt and pepper to taste. Set aside.

To serve: Preheat oven to 325 degrees. Divide arugula and arrange in center of 4 plates. Place green beans on both sides of plate so they extend from center in a fanlike pattern; arrange zucchini in a similar fanlike pattern at bottom of plate.

Reheat langoustines in preheated oven for about 3 minutes. Heat citrus vinaigrette over low heat, whisking, until warm. Arrange shelled langoustines at top end of plates and place one whole langoustine in center of each plate, with claws forming a triangle at top. Place 1 basil leaf on each side of langoustine and a cherry tomato near both clusters of beans. Coat langoustines with warm citrus vinaigrette and sprinkle with basil chiffonade. Serve immediately.

Makes 4 servings

Overleaf: Nouvelle cuisine often recalls the style of Japanese food arrangement. In this dish by Jacques Chibois the steamed langoustines are coated with hot citrus vinaigrette and sprinkled with basil chiffonade.

Pierre Gagnaire

TAMPURA DE LANGOUSTINES, POMMES DE TERRE SAUTEES AU BEURRE CLARIFIE, BEURRE FONDU A LA CANNELLE ET CIBOULETTE

LANGOUSTINE TEMPURA WITH CHIVE AND CINNAMON BUTTER

LANGOUSTINE TEMPURA:

8	large langoustines or shrimp, shelled
½	cup heavy cream
1	large or 2 small green cabbage leaves
2	small baking potatoes, peeled, sliced ⅛-inch thick, and soaked in cold water overnight
½	cup unsalted butter, clarified, plus 1 tablespoon butter, at room temperature
2	cups vegetable oil
½	cup flour
2	radishes, thinly sliced, in 1 tablespoon safflower oil

CHIVE AND CINNAMON BUTTER:

2	tablespoons cold water
	Pinch of salt
¼	teaspoon cinnamon
4	tablespoons cold unsalted butter, cut into pieces
1	tablespoon fresh chives, finely chopped

122

Prepare langoustine tempura: Preheat oven to 375 degrees. In a medium bowl, place langoustines and heavy cream; set aside. Blanch cabbage in 2 cups boiling, salted water for 2 to 3 minutes. Transfer to a bowl of ice water to cool; drain and set aside.

Drain and dry potato slices and coat with clarified butter. Arrange potatoes, in a single layer, on a large, heavy baking sheet and bake in preheated oven for 15 to 20 minutes or until crisp and golden. Remove from oven and keep warm.

Prepare chive and cinnamon butter: In a small, heavy saucepan, heat water, salt, and cinnamon over low heat. Whisk in butter, a few pieces at a time.

When butter is incorporated, add chives. Remove from heat and keep warm.

To serve: In a heavy skillet or saucepan, heat oil to 370 degrees. One at a time, remove langoustines from cream and coat lightly with flour; deep-fry in hot oil for 1 to 2 minutes. With a slotted spoon, remove langoustines and cut into small pieces; salt to taste. In a heavy saucepan, heat 1 tablespoon butter over low heat. Add cabbage leaves and cook for 3 to 5 minutes without browning.

Place cabbage in center of 2 heated plates. Arrange potato slices on top and surround with pieces of langoustine. Decorate plates with radish slivers and a ribbon of chive and cinnamon butter.

Makes 2 servings

Pierre Gagnaire

CONSOMME GLACE GERMINY, FILET DE PIGEON AU JUS DE BETTERAVE

SQUAB BREASTS WITH GERMINY MOUSSE AND BEET CREAM SAUCE

GERMINY MOUSSE:

¾	cup gelatinous beef or veal stock
3	egg yolks
1	tablespoon port
¼	cup heavy cream, stiffly beaten

SQUAB BREASTS AND VEGETABLES:

1	carrot, cut into ¼-inch matchsticks
1	cup boiling stock or salted water
2	large spinach leaves, stemmed and finely shredded
¼	teaspoon soy sauce
	Salt and freshly ground pepper
2	1⅓-pound squabs, breasts removed, or ½ pound squab breasts
1	teaspoon unsalted butter
1	shallot, finely chopped
⅛	teaspoon coarse salt

Preceding overleaf: Pierre Gagnaire's langoustine tempura.

BEET CREAM SAUCE:

⅓   cup heavy cream

1   small canned beet, drained and crushed

Prepare Germiny mousse: In a medium saucepan, heat stock. In a small bowl, beat egg yolks until well combined, but not frothy. Slowly pour hot stock into yolks, whisking constantly, until blended. Return mixture to saucepan and cook over low heat, stirring constantly with a wooden spoon, for about 6 minutes or until mixture is thick enough to coat the spoon. Strain mixture into a medium bowl and refrigerate, stirring from time to time, until well chilled and thick. When cold, stir in port and gently fold in whipped cream. Cover and refrigerate until serving time.

Prepare squab breasts and vegetables: Cook carrot in boiling stock for about 10 minutes or until tender when pierced with a knife. Drain, refresh under cold water, and set aside.

Toss spinach with soy sauce and a pinch of salt; set aside.

Place a small skillet over medium-high heat. Add squab breasts, skin side down, and sauté for 2 to 3 minutes on each side or until nicely browned. (Do not overcook breasts, as they should remain quite pink.) Season lightly with salt and transfer to a plate.

In the same skillet, melt butter over medium heat. Add shallot and cook, stirring, for 2 to 3 minutes or until shallot is soft but not brown; set aside.

Prepare beet cream sauce: In a small saucepan, combine cream and crushed beet; bring to a boil over high heat. Strain mixture, pressing lightly on beet to extract all liquid.

To serve: Using 2 spoons dipped in hot water, place 2 large scoops of mousse on each of 2 plates. Place spinach and carrot sticks on plates and sprinkle carrots with coarse salt. Slice each squab breast in half lengthwise and arrange attractively on plates. Drizzle with shallot sauce and sprinkle with freshly ground pepper. Spoon beet cream sauce around the edge of each plate and serve.

Makes 2 servings

Squab breasts are served with Germiny mousse and beet cream sauce in this recipe by Pierre Gagnaire.

Georges Blanc

GOURMANDISE GLACEE AUX GROSEILLES
MERINGUES WITH RED CURRANT SORBET AND RED FRUITS

RED CURRANT SORBET:

1⅓	cups soda water
1½	cups granulated sugar
2¼	pounds fresh red currants, stems removed
	Juice of 2 lemons

MERINGUE:

5	large egg whites
⅔	cup granulated sugar
1	cup powdered sugar, sifted

CUSTARD:

1	cup milk
1	vanilla bean, split
3	egg yolks
¼	cup granulated sugar
1	tablespoon plus 2 teaspoons cornstarch, sifted

RED CURRANT SAUCE:

1	pound fresh red currants, stems removed
	Powdered sugar, to taste
1½	pints wild strawberries or raspberries or a combination of the two
	Fresh mint leaves and red currants

124

Prepare red currant sorbet: In a small saucepan, bring soda water and sugar to a boil over high heat. Cook until sugar is dissolved. Transfer to a heat-proof bowl and refrigerate until cold. Purée currants in a food processor. Strain juice into cold sugar syrup and add lemon juice. Pour mixture into an ice cream machine and freeze according to the manufacturer's instructions.

Prepare meringue: Preheat oven to 300 degrees. Butter and flour 2 baking sheets. Using a 3-inch round cookie or biscuit cutter as a guide, outline 8 evenly spaced circles on each baking sheet.

With an electric mixer, beat egg whites until soft peaks form. Add 4 teaspoons granulated sugar and continue beating until stiff peaks form. Combine remaining granulated sugar with powdered sugar and gradually fold them into beaten whites.

Spoon meringue into a large pastry bag fitted with a ½-inch round tip. Pipe meringue into outlined circles, beginning in centers and spiraling meringue out to rims; you should have 16 circles of the same size. Bake meringues in preheated oven for about 1 hour or until lightly browned.

Prepare custard: In a medium saucepan, combine milk and vanilla bean; bring slowly to a boil. In a medium bowl, whisk egg yolks with sugar until pale and fluffy. Add cornstarch and whisk until blended. Slowly pour hot milk into beaten yolks, whisking constantly. Return mixture to saucepan and cook over medium heat, whisking constantly, for about 2 minutes or until boiling. Remove vanilla bean. Pour custard into a shallow bowl, cover, and refrigerate until chilled.

Prepare sauce: Purée red currants in a food processor. Strain juice into a bowl and whisk in powdered sugar to taste; refrigerate.

To serve: Spread chilled custard over half of the meringue rounds and arrange berries on top. Spread remaining meringues with sorbet. Pour currant sauce onto 8 dessert plates and place a sorbet-spread meringue on each. Top each one with a berry-topped meringue. Garnish with mint leaves and red currants and serve immediately.

Makes 8 servings

Georges Blanc purées red currants to make a sauce for gourmandise glacée aux groseilles.

Jacques Chibois

LE DORADE ROYALE AU BASILIC ET AUX PETITES AUBERGINES

SEA BREAM WITH BASIL AND TINY EGGPLANTS

BASIL SAUCE:

2	tablespoons minced shallots
½	cup white wine
½	cup chicken stock
¼	teaspoon soy sauce
	Grated zest of 1 lemon
7	tablespoons cold unsalted butter, cut into pieces
¼	teaspoon walnut oil
¼	teaspoon lemon juice
12	large fresh basil leaves, cut widthwise into thin strips
	Salt and freshly ground pepper

FISH AND EGGPLANT:

2	pounds sea bream, cut into 4 fillets of equal size, or substitute other saltwater fish
4	tiny eggplants plus 1 tiny eggplant, peeled and diced
2	tablespoons olive oil
2	tablespoons finely chopped onion
¼	teaspoon minced garlic
½	teaspoon walnut oil
2	tablespoons red pepper, cut into ⅛-inch dice
2	tablespoons unsalted butter
2	large potatoes, boiled and cut into 16 slices

126

Prepare basil sauce: In a small, heavy saucepan, combine shallots and white wine. Cook over medium heat until liquid is reduced to a few tablespoons. Add chicken stock, soy sauce, and grated lemon zest, and cook over medium heat until reduced by half. Whisk in butter, a few pieces at a time. Add walnut oil, lemon juice, and basil leaves; season with salt and pepper to taste. Reserve.

Prepare fish and eggplant: Wash and dry fish fillets; wrap in a clean cloth and refrigerate.

Preheat oven to 350 degrees. Cut 4 eggplants in half and remove a small amount of flesh from each; chop flesh and reserve. Blanch eggplant halves in 3 to 4 cups boiling salted water for about 5 minutes. Remove with a slotted spoon and arrange in an ovenproof dish. Cook diced eggplant and reserved eggplant flesh in boiling salted water for about 2 minutes. Remove and drain. In a heavy saucepan, heat 1 tablespoon olive oil. Add onion and sauté until lightly colored; add eggplant pieces, garlic, walnut oil, and red pepper. Cook over medium heat, stirring with a wooden spoon, for 5 to 8 minutes. Spoon mixture into 4 eggplant halves. Place eggplants and potatoes in preheated oven and bake for 6 to 10 minutes or until warm. In a large skillet, heat 2 tablespoons butter and remaining olive oil. Add fish fillets and sauté for about 3 minutes on each side.

To serve: Place a fish fillet in the center of each of 4 heated plates. Arrange a filled eggplant half at top edge of plate and cover with an empty eggplant half. Arrange 2 slices of potato, on each side of fish, and spoon warm sauce over top. Serve immediately.

Makes 4 servings

Sea bream with basil and tiny eggplants make an elegant dish when prepared by Jacques Chibois.

Jacques Chibois

LE CROUSTILLANT DE FRAISES DES BOIS AU COULIS DE RHUBARBE

HONEY CRISPS WITH WILD STRAWBERRIES, WHIPPED CREAM, AND RHUBARB SAUCE

CANDIED LIME ZESTS:

	Zests from 2 limes, cut into thin julienne
¾	cup granulated sugar
½	cup water

RHUBARB SAUCE:

½	pound fresh rhubarb, trimmed, peeled, and sliced
3	tablespoons granulated sugar
¼	cup water

HONEY CRISPS:

2	tablespoons unsalted butter, softened
⅓	cup powdered sugar, sifted
2	tablespoons light honey
⅓	cup flour, sifted
1	egg white
	Pinch of ginger
	Powdered sugar, for sifting
1	cup heavy cream, beaten until stiff with 1½ tablespoons powdered sugar, or to taste
¾	pound wild strawberries or 2 pints ripe strawberries, hulled and quartered

128

Prepare candied lime zests: Blanch lime zests in a saucepan of boiling water; drain and repeat, blanching and draining twice more. In a medium saucepan, combine sugar and water and cook over high heat for about 3 minutes or until sugar is dissolved. Add blanched zests and cook over medium heat for about 25 minutes or until lightly candied. Transfer zests to a lightly oiled rack and separate with a fork; cool.

Prepare rhubarb sauce: In a medium saucepan, combine rhubarb, sugar, and water. Cover and cook over medium-high heat for 5 minutes. Uncover and continue cooking, stirring from time to time, for about 7 minutes or until rhubarb is very tender. Purée rhubarb in a blender or food processor. Strain into a small bowl, cover, and refrigerate until serving time.

Prepare honey crisps: Preheat oven to 425 degrees. In a medium bowl, cream butter. One at a time, add powdered sugar, honey, flour, egg white, and ginger; beat after each addition until ingredient is fully incorporated.

Spoon 6 scant teaspoons of batter, about 1½ inches apart, onto an ungreased, nonstick baking sheet. Moisten back of a small spoon and, using a gentle circular motion, spread batter to form very thin circles, about 3 inches in diameter. Bake for about 3 minutes or until golden brown. With a metal spatula, carefully transfer wafers to a rack to cool. (If wafers become brittle, reheat briefly in the oven to soften.) Let baking sheet cool, then repeat with remaining batter; you should have 24 wafers.

To serve: Sift powdered sugar over 6 wafers. Spread remaining 18 wafers with whipped cream (or pipe whipped cream onto wafers with a pastry bag fitted with a medium star tip). Cover each cream-topped wafer with strawberries. Spoon rhubarb purée onto 6 dessert plates and stack 3 of the cream-and-strawberry-covered wafers on each. Top each stack with a powdered-sugar-coated wafer. Garnish with candied lime zests..

Makes 6 servings

Old-fashioned honey crisps are transformed with wild strawberries and rhubarb sauce by Jacques Chibois.

Michel Trama

PETIT SALE DE CANARD AUX LENTILLES
SALT-CURED DUCK LEGS WITH VEGETABLES AND LENTILS

6	large duck legs, about ½ pound each (from foie gras ducks)
¼	cup coarse salt
1	medium carrot, thinly sliced, plus 3 medium carrots, cut into large ovals or thickly sliced, plus 1 carrot, finely diced
1	onion, studded with 3 cloves
1	bouquet garni, made with celery, leek, bay leaves, parsley stems, and thyme

1	star anise pod
1	quart plus 2 cups water
3	medium turnips, cut into large ovals or sixths
3	red-skinned potatoes, cut into large ovals or sixths
1	tablespoon goose fat
2	shallots, finely chopped
1	ounce pancetta, cut into julienne
2	Italian plum tomatoes, peeled, seeded, and coarsely chopped
2	garlic cloves, finely chopped
½	cup green lentils
1	bouquet garni
	Salt and freshly ground pepper
6	large cabbage leaves, central ribs removed

Michel Trama serves duck legs with vegetable-and-lentil stuffed cabbage leaf.

Place duck legs in a large earthenware dish and rub with salt. Cover and refrigerate, turning occasionally, for 12 hours or overnight.

In a large saucepan, combine thinly sliced carrot, onion, bouquet garni, star anise, and 1 quart water. Bring to a boil, cover partially, and simmer over medium heat for 1 hour. Strain liquid into a large ovenproof casserole.

Preheat oven to 350 degrees.

Rinse salt from duck legs with cold water and pat dry with paper towels. Add duck to casserole and bring to a boil over medium heat. Cover casserole and bake in preheated oven for 1 hour. Add carrot ovals, turnips, and potatoes and bake for about 20 minutes or until duck and vegetables are tender.

In a large saucepan, melt goose fat. Add diced carrot, shallots, pancetta, tomatoes, and garlic, and cook over low heat, stirring occasionally, for 12 to 15 minutes, or until vegetables are soft but not brown. Add lentils, bouquet garni, and 2 cups water. Bring to a boil over high heat and skim. Reduce heat to medium, cover, and simmer for about 30 minutes or until lentils are tender. Add 1 teaspoon salt halfway through cooking time. Drain lentils, discard bouquet garni, and season to taste with additional salt and pepper.

Blanch cabbage leaves in a large pot of boiling, salted water for about 4 minutes or until tender. Drain, refresh under cold water, and drain again. Pat dry with paper towels.

Spread cabbage leaves on a work surface and divide lentil mixture among them. Fold cabbage leaves over lentils to form neat packages.

To serve: Rewarm cabbage packages in a large steamer for about 5 minutes or until heated through. Reheat duck and vegetables, if necessary. Place a cabbage package on each plate, along with a duck leg and a portion of vegetables. Serve immediately.

Makes 6 servings

Ed. note: The duck legs called for in this recipe can be ordered from D'Artagnan, Inc., 399-419 St. Paul Avenue, Jersey City, New Jersey 07306, (201) 792-0748.

Michel Trama

FEUILLANTINE AU CHOCOLAT
CHOCOLATE MOUSSE SQUARES

CHOCOLATE MOUSSE:
5	tablespoons unsalted butter
1½	ounces imported semisweet chocolate
½	cup unsweetened Dutch process cocoa
2	egg yolks
¼	cup sugar
2	tablespoons strong brewed coffee
2	tablespoons water
½	cup heavy cream, whipped until firm

CHOCOLATE SQUARES:
2½	ounces semisweet chocolate

Prepare chocolate mousse: In a double boiler, combine butter, chocolate, and cocoa; heat until thoroughly melted. Mix well to combine.

Meanwhile, with an electric mixer, beat egg yolks and sugar until pale and thick. Beat in coffee and water, then beat in hot chocolate mixture. Turn the mixer on high speed and beat in whipped cream. Cover and refrigerate for at least 2 hours.

Prepare chocolate squares: In a double boiler, melt 2½ ounces chocolate. Remove from heat and let cool slightly.

Place a sheet of parchment paper on a cookie tray and weight down ends of paper securely. With a pencil and a ruler, draw an 8-by-10-inch rectangle.

Pour melted chocolate into center of rectangle and use a spatula to spread it as evenly as possible, following the outline you have drawn. Set aside in a cool place to harden; do not refrigerate. When chocolate is nearly firm, use a sharp knife to score 12 rectangles of equal size. Let chocolate harden completely.

Carefully peel chocolate rectangles from parchment paper. Place a chocolate rectangle on each plate, top with a large dollop of chocolate mousse, and cover with remaining rectangles.

Makes 6 servings

Ed. note: Use the best semisweet chocolate you can find for this dessert.

131

Overleaf: Chocolate mousse squares from Michel Trama.

Jacques Maximin

FLEURS DE COURGETTE AUX TRUFFES

STUFFED ZUCCHINI BLOSSOMS WITH TRUFFLES AND FRESH HERBS

3½	slices white bread, crusts removed
1	cup heavy cream
16	zucchini with blossoms attached
¼	cup extra virgin olive oil
10	large, fresh basil leaves
1	extra large egg
	Salt and freshly ground pepper
½	cup water
⅔	cup cold unsalted butter
1	1½-ounce fresh truffle, peeled and thinly sliced
1	teaspoon truffle juice, optional
½	cup crème fraîche, beaten until stiff
1	ounce fresh chervil leaves
1	ounce fresh tarragon leaves

In a medium bowl, soak bread in heavy cream; set aside. Leaving blossoms intact, trim zucchini to 4-inch lengths. Finely chop trimmings. In a small skillet, heat 2 teaspoons olive oil. Add zucchini trimmings and sauté over medium-high heat, stirring, for about 2 minutes or until tender. In a blender, combine zucchini trimmings, basil leaves, egg, and soaked bread; purée until smooth. Scrape mixture into a bowl, cover, and refrigerate.

Preheat oven to 400 degrees.

Open zucchini blossoms very gently and remove centers; try to avoid tearing. Fill a large bowl with cold water and a few ice cubes. Bring a large saucepan of salted water to a boil, add zucchini, and blanch for 10 seconds. Drain and immediately place in ice water. Drain zucchini and blot dry with paper towels. With a small paring knife, carefully cut zucchini lengthwise into ⅜-inch-thick slices; do not cut through blossoms.

Grease a large baking sheet with 1½ tablespoons olive oil. Spoon basil mixture into a pastry bag fitted with a very small round tip. Carefully open each zucchini blossom just enough to insert tip of pastry bag, and fill three quarters full with basil mixture. Twist

flower tips to enclose mixture and place on greased baking sheet. Brush zucchini with remaining olive oil and sprinkle with salt and pepper. Cover with aluminum foil and bake for 30 minutes or until tender when pierced with a fork.

Meanwhile, bring water to a boil in a medium saucepan. Add a pinch of salt and pepper and reduce heat to medium. Whisk in butter, 2 tablespoons at a time. Remove from heat and add sliced truffle and truffle juice; set aside to infuse.

To serve: Drain zucchini on paper towels and place 4 on each plate; press lightly into a fanlike pattern. With a slotted spoon, remove truffle slices from sauce and scatter over zucchini. Bring sauce to a boil over medium heat and whisk in crème fraîche. Season with salt and pepper to taste and pour sauce over zucchini. Sprinkle with chervil and tarragon and serve immediately.

Makes 4 servings

Michel Trama

TERRINE DE POIREAUX A LA VINAIGRETTE ET JULIENNE DE TRUFFES

LEEK TERRINE WITH VINAIGRETTE AND JULIENNE OF TRUFFLES

LEEK TERRINE:

24	to 30 leeks, washed, trimmed, and cut into approximately 10-inch lengths
6	to 8 quarts water
	Salt and freshly ground pepper

JULIENNE OF TRUFFLES:

2	fresh or preserved truffles (about 1½ ounces)

TRUFFLE VINAIGRETTE:

	Reserved truffle peels
	Juice of 1½ lemons
¼	teaspoon salt
⅛	teaspoon freshly ground pepper
1	cup safflower or vegetable oil
¼	cup boiling water

Preceding overleaf: Jacques Maximin is credited with being the first to use zucchini blossoms in nouvelle cuisine. Here he stuffs them and serves them with fresh herbs.

Prepare leek terrine: Divide leeks into bunches of 6 and tie each with kitchen string.

In a large enamel or stainless-steel pot, bring water and 1 tablespoon salt to a boil. Add leeks; return to a boil and cook for 10 to 15 minutes. Transfer leeks to a large bowl of ice water to cool. Then drain, squeeze out any excess water, and untie bunches.

Line a 10-by-4-by-3-inch terrine mold with aluminum foil, leaving a 1½-inch overhang on all sides. Place a layer of about 4 to 5 leeks in bottom of terrine, with white parts at one end. Season with salt and pepper. Layer more leeks on top; this time, the white ends should rest on the green tops of the preceding layer. Repeat alternate layering, seasoning each layer with salt and pepper, until terrine is full. Fold overlapping aluminum foil to cover leeks.

Place a board the size of the interior of the mold on top of leeks. Invert mold, with board in place, onto a dish and place a weight on top of terrine. Refrigerate for at least 6 hours. This will compress the leeks and extract excess water.

Prepare julienne of truffles: With a small paring knife, peel truffles and reserve peel for truffle vinaigrette. Slice truffles ⅛-inch thick, then cut into 1- to 1½-inch strips.

Prepare truffle vinaigrette: In a blender or food processor fitted with a metal blade, process truffle peels, lemon juice, salt, and pepper. Add oil and process to form an emulsion. Add water and process for 1 second longer.

To serve: Remove aluminum-foil-wrapped leeks from terrine; unwrap and invert onto a cutting board. With a large, sharp knife, slice terrine. Spoon truffle vinaigrette over each slice and garnish with julienne of truffles.

Makes 6 servings

Michel Trama layers cooked leeks—white bases on green tops—in a terrine and serves slices chilled.

Jean-Marie Amat

SALADE D'HUITRES AU CAVIAR

SPINACH-WRAPPED OYSTERS WITH BLACK CAVIAR

24	large fresh spinach leaves
24	fresh oysters, preferably Belon
3	tablespoons vinaigrette
2	small shallots, very finely chopped
3½	ounces black caviar
½	lemon

Blanch spinach leaves in a large pot of boiling salted water for 10 seconds; refresh under cold running water and drain well.

Preheat oven to 350 degrees.

Shuck oysters and place in a medium saucepan with their liquor. Place the saucepan over medium heat and warm the oysters for about 5 minutes or until their edges begin to curl. With a slotted spoon, transfer oysters to a bowl of cold water to cool; drain well.

Wrap each oyster in a spinach leaf and place in a small baking dish. Stir 1 tablespoon of oyster liquor into the vinaigrette and spoon this sauce over the oysters. Sprinkle with shallots. Warm oysters in the oven with the door open for about 1 minute.

Arrange 6 spinach-wrapped oysters on each plate. Top each one with a bit of sauce. Place a small spoonful of caviar on each oyster and top with a drop of lemon juice. Serve immediately.

Makes 4 servings

Jean-Marie Amat recommends fresh Belon oysters for this dish.

André and Arnaud Daguin

LA CHARTREUSE DE PERDREAU

CHARTREUSE OF YOUNG PARTRIDGE

1	small green cabbage, quartered through core so leaves remain intact
½	pound fresh, lightly salted unsmoked bacon, in one piece
1	tablespoon plus 2 teaspoons goose fat
1	onion, finely chopped
1	leek, washed, trimmed, and finely chopped
1	carrot, finely chopped, plus 1 carrot, peeled
2	cups chicken stock
1	andouillette (chitterling sausage) or seasoned pork sausage, poached and sliced as thin as possible
¼	pound boudin (blood sausage), poached and sliced as thin as possible
¾	to 1 pound young partridge, cleaned and cut in half lengthwise
1	tablespoon butter

The Daguins' chartreuse of young partridge.

Preheat oven to 275 degrees. Blanch cabbage in boiling salted water for about 2 minutes. With a slotted spoon, transfer cabbage to a plate and reserve. With a sharp knife, remove bacon rind, then cut two thin, lengthwise slices and reserve. Finely chop remaining bacon.

In a heavy roasting pan, melt 2 teaspoons goose fat over medium heat. Add chopped bacon, onion, leek, and chopped carrot and sauté for about 5 minutes or until rich brown in color. Place 4 sections of cabbage on top and add chicken stock; it should cover about half of cabbage. Bring to a boil. Remove from heat and transfer to preheated oven. Cook, covered, for 2 to 3 hours. (The longer the cabbage braises, the more flavor it will add to the dish.)

Meanwhile, butter 2 small stainless-steel or ovenproof bowls, 6 inches in diameter and 2½ to 3 inches deep. Place a slice of reserved bacon across bottom and extending up sides of each bowl. With a lemon zester, make channels in sides of peeled carrot. Thinly slice carrot and blanch in boiling, salted water for about 3 minutes. Remove with a slotted spoon and line bottom of bowls with carrot slices, covering bacon, if necessary. Line bowls, layering over carrots, with andouillette and boudin slices. Refrigerate.

Remove cabbage from roasting pan and increase oven temperature to 375 degrees. Strain cooking juices into a small bowl; press liquid from braised cabbage and reserve.

In a heavy skillet, heat 1 tablespoon goose fat over medium to medium-high heat. Add partridge halves and cook for about 5 minutes or until browned on both sides. Remove partridge and add reserved braising liquid to skillet. Cook over medium to high heat until reduced to ½ cup. Reserve.

Place a layer of cabbage in each prepared bowl and then add half a partridge, skin side down. Add a second layer of cabbage, covering partridge and reaching top of bowls. Cover tightly with aluminum foil and bake in preheated oven for 20 minutes.

Remove from oven, uncover, and pour off any excess liquid. To unmold, invert onto a serving dish. Coat with reduced braising liquid and serve.

Makes 2 servings

139

LE STEAK DE CARPE DE BRENNE AU CHINON ROUGE

MARINATED CARP STEAKS WITH RED WINE

MARINADE AND FISH:
- ¾ cup olive oil
- ½ teaspoon coarsely cracked black pepper
- 10 coriander seeds
  - Pinch of quatre épices
- 2 bay leaves
- 4 pounds carp, filleted, skin intact, bones reserved and chopped

SAUCE:
- 5 tablespoons unsalted butter
- 2 shallots, chopped
  - Reserved carp bones
- 2 ¾ cups Chinon or other light, dry red wine
  - Bouquet garni made with celery
  - Pinch of cinnamon
  - Pinch of sugar

VEGETABLE GARNISHES:
- 1 small savoy cabbage, large leaves deribbed, coarsely shredded
- 7 tablespoons unsalted butter
- ⅓ pound bacon, cut into thin strips
  - Salt and freshly ground pepper
  - Coarse salt
- 4 small red potatoes
- 12 pearl onions
- ¼ teaspoon sugar
- ½ cup water
- 1 tablespoon vegetable oil
- 8 wild mushrooms, such as chanterelles or pleurottes, cut into pieces if large

Prepare marinade: In a large nonmetallic dish, combine ½ cup olive oil, cracked black pepper, coriander, quatre épices, and bay leaves. Add fish and turn to coat well. Cover and refrigerate overnight, turning occasionally.

Prepare sauce: In a medium saucepan, melt 1 tablespoon butter. Add shallots and carp bones and cook over medium heat, stirring frequently, for about 5 minutes or until shallots soften and bones whiten. Add 2 cups Chinon and bouquet garni and simmer over medium heat for 20 minutes. Strain stock into a saucepan, pressing hard on the solids to extract all liquid.

Bring stock to a boil and cook for about 20 minutes or until reduced to 6 tablespoons. Meanwhile, in a small saucepan, combine remaining Chinon, cinnamon, and sugar and bring to a boil. Cook for about 12 minutes or until reduced to ¼ cup. Combine the two reductions and set aside.

Prepare vegetable garnishes: Preheat oven to 350 degrees. Blanch cabbage leaves in boiling salted water for 2 minutes; drain well. In a medium skillet, melt 1 tablespoon butter. Add bacon and sauté over medium-high heat for about 6 minutes or until bacon begins to brown. Reduce heat to medium, add cabbage, and cook, tossing frequently, for about 8 minutes or until cabbage is tender. Season with salt and pepper to taste.

Pour coarse salt into a small baking dish and set potatoes on top; bake for about 50 minutes or until tender.

Blanch pearl onions in boiling salted water for 30 seconds; drain and peel. In a small, heavy saucepan, melt 1 tablespoon butter. Add onions, sugar, and a pinch of salt. Pour in water, cover, and cook over medium heat for about 15 minutes or until onions are just tender. Uncover and continue cooking, shaking pan frequently, for about 10 minutes, or until water has evaporated and onions are nicely browned and caramelized. Season to taste.

In a medium skillet, melt 2 tablespoons butter and oil. Add mushrooms and sauté over medium-high heat for about 3 minutes or until tender.

In a medium skillet, melt remaining butter. Peel

Jean Bardet garnishes carp steaks with a mix of cabbage, bacon, potatoes, onions, and wild mushrooms.

potatoes and cook over medium heat, tossing, for about 5 minutes or until heated through.

To serve: Heat ¼ cup olive oil in a large skillet. Season carp with salt and pepper and cut each fillet in half crosswise. Add fish to skillet, skin side down, and fry for about 5 minutes on each side or until nicely browned. Reheat all vegetable garnishes. Bring reserved sauce to a boil and whisk in the remaining 4 tablespoons butter, 1 tablespoon at a time. Season with salt and pepper to taste. Place a carp steak, skin side up, on each plate and surround with vegetables. Spoon sauce over fish or pass separately in a sauceboat.

Makes 4 servings

Jean Bardet

LE CIVET GOURMAND DE HOMARD ET LANGOUSTINES AU QUARTS DE CHAUME ET GINGEMBRE

LOBSTER WITH GINGER BUTTER SAUCE

1	2½-pound live lobster
1	small zucchini
1	medium carrot
1	medium turnip
¾	cup Quarts de Chaume or Sauternes*
2	inch piece of fresh ginger, peeled and sliced (about ¼ cup)
3	tablespoons heavy cream
¾	cup cold unsalted butter
	Salt and freshly ground pepper
	Juice of ½ lime
8	raw langoustines, shelled and deveined
	Grated lime zest
4	sprigs of fresh dill

Bring water to a boil in a large steamer. Add lobster and steam over high heat for 8 minutes. Remove lobster and detach tail section. Return claws, legs,

and head to pot and steam for 2 minutes longer; let cool.

With a small, sharp knife, carve zucchini into 4 olive shapes of even size; try to leave as much of the skin as possible. Carve the carrot and turnip into 4 "olives" each; they should be the same size as the zucchini.

Bring a medium saucepan of salted water to a boil. Add vegetables and cook until just tender, about 5 minutes for zucchini and 8 minutes for the turnip and carrot; refresh under cold water.

In a small, heavy saucepan, combine ½ cup wine and the ginger. Cook over medium-low heat for about 25 minutes or until wine reduces to 2 teaspoons. Add cream and bring to a boil over medium high heat. Reduce heat to low and whisk in butter, 2 tablespoons at a time. Season to taste with salt, pepper, and lime juice. Remove from heat.

Preheat oven to 500 degrees. Remove meat from the lobster tail, claws, and forelegs. Cut tail into 16 thin slices; remove and discard intestinal tract. Place lobster meat in a shallow baking dish and add remaining ¼ cup wine.

Place langoustines in a lightly buttered baking dish and season with salt and pepper. Bake for 1 minute. Reheat lobster in the oven with the door open. Reheat vegetables in a steamer. Place sauce over medium heat and whisk constantly until warm. Remove from heat and strain through a fine-mesh strainer, pressing hard on the ginger to extract juices.

141

To serve: Drain lobster meat and divide evenly among 4 plates. Place 2 langoustines and 1 of each vegetable "olive" on each plate. Lightly coat shellfish with sauce and sprinkle with grated lime zest. Garnish each serving with a sprig of dill.

Makes 4 servings

Ed. note: The original version of this recipe calls for Quarts de Chaume, a sweet white wine from Anjou. If you cannot find this wine, substitute an equal amount of Sauternes. If langoustines are unavailable, substitute large shrimps.

Overleaf: For this lobster dish Jean Bardet prepares a ginger butter sauce.

Jean Bardet

LE PETIT RAGOUT FIN D'HUITRES SUR UNE MOUSSE LEGERE AU CRESSON RENFORCEE AU MUSCADET

FINE OYSTER RAGOUT ON WATERCRESS MOUSSE WITH MUSCADET

OYSTER RAGOUT:
16   fresh oysters, shells removed and liquor reserved
¼   cup Muscadet (remainder of bottle chilled to drink with ragout)
     Pinch of cayenne pepper

BEURRE BLANC:
3   tablespoons minced shallots
½   teaspoon crushed white peppercorns
3   tablespoons white wine vinegar
3   tablespoons oyster liquid with Muscadet
¾   cup cold unsalted butter, cut into small pieces

WATERCRESS MOUSSE:
2   quarts water
½   teaspoon salt
1   bunch watercress, trimmed
     Reserved beurre blanc

Prepare oysters: In a small saucepan, combine oysters, reserved liquor, and Muscadet. Set aside until serving time.

Prepare beurre blanc: In a small, heavy saucepan, combine shallots, pepper, vinegar, and oyster liquor. Cook over low heat until liquor is reduced to 1 tablespoon (shallots should not color). Add butter, a few pieces at a time, and cook over medium heat, whisking constantly, until creamy. Strain through a fine mesh sieve. Set aside about ½ cup sauce and keep warm until serving time. Reserve remaining sauce for watercress mousse.

Prepare watercress mousse: In a medium saucepan, bring water to a boil and add salt. Add watercress and blanch for 3 minutes. Transfer watercress to a bowl of ice water to cool. Drain and place watercress in a blender. Process until finely puréed and add reserved beurre blanc.

To serve: Heat oysters over low heat until liquid barely begins to bubble and simmer for 30 seconds. Divide mousse among 4 hot plates and spoon 4 swirls of warm beurre blanc onto each. With a slotted spoon, remove oysters from saucepan and place one on each swirl of beurre blanc. Sprinkle the cayenne over each oyster and serve immediately with remaining Muscadet.   Makes 4 servings

Facing page: Jean Bardet steeps oysters in Muscadet, then serves with two sauces.

Didier Clement

FILET DE LIEVRE EN AIGUILLETTES AUX CLEMENTINES

HARE FILLETS WITH CLEMENTINES

1   to 2 ounces lard, cut into ¼-by-1½-inch strips
2   large saddles of hare, boned, with bones reserved and chopped
¼   cup safflower oil
¾   cup unsalted butter
2   tablespoons chopped shallots
1   carrot, peeled and chopped
1   rib celery, chopped
1   sprig fresh thyme
1   bay leaf
1   quart dry red wine
1   quart hare or beef stock
½   cup sugar
⅓   cup water
4   small clementines, peeled and divided into quarters
4   ounces fresh noodles, cooked and drained
4   small Golden Delicious apples, peeled, cored, and thinly sliced

(Recipe continued on following page.)

145

Didier Clement's hare fillets with clementines.

With a larding needle, thread strips of lard throughout hare fillets. In a large skillet, heat 2 tablespoons oil and 3 tablespoons butter. Add reserved bones and brown. Add shallots, carrot, celery, thyme, and bay leaf. Continue to cook over medium heat for about 5 minutes or until vegetables soften and color slightly. Add wine and cook over medium to high heat until reduced to about 1 cup of jellylike glaze. Add stock and boil until reduced to about 1 cup; strain and reserve. (You should have about 1 cup strained liquid.)

In a heavy enamel or stainless-steel saucepan, combine sugar and water. Cook over medium heat until thick, syrupy, and barely colored. Glaze clementine sections with syrup and reserve.

In a bowl, toss noodles and apples. In a heavy skillet, heat 2 tablespoons butter. Add noodle mixture and cook over low to medium heat until mixture is lightly browned and resembles a pancake. Keep warm and reserve.

In a heavy skillet, heat 4 tablespoons butter and 2 tablespoons oil. Add hare fillets and sauté over high heat for 5 to 8 minutes or until browned on all sides, but still rare. Transfer meat to a cutting board and degrease pan. Add reserved wine-stock mixture and deglaze. With skillet over low heat, whisk in 3 tablespoons butter; do not let sauce boil.

To serve: With a sharp knife, slice fillets lengthwise. Spoon a little sauce onto each of 4 heated plates and arrange meat on top. Divide noodle pancake into 4 portions and place one in center of each plate. Decorate with glazed clementines.

Makes 4 servings

Didier Clement

MI-FIGUE MI-RAISIN AU LAIT D'AMANDES
FIGS AND GRAPES
WITH ALMOND ICE CREAM

ALMOND MILK:
- ¼ cup soft almond paste
- ¾ cup boiled and slightly cooled water

ALMOND ICE CREAM:
- 6 large egg yolks
- 2 cups milk
- ¼ cup sugar
- 1 cup almond milk

FIGS:
- 4 cups sugar
- 4 cups water
- 16 fresh figs
- 16 large Muscat grapes, peeled

Prepare almond milk: In a food processor or blender, process almond paste and water until well combined.

Prepare almond ice cream: In a large bowl, whisk egg yolks for about 1 minute or until light in color. In a heavy saucepan, combine milk and sugar. Cook over medium heat, stirring with a wooden spoon, just until milk begins to boil. Pour about ½ cup hot milk mixture into egg yolks and whisk well. Whisking constantly, pour egg-milk mixture into saucepan and cook over low heat for a few minutes or until mixture thickens enough to coat the back of a spoon. Remove from heat, whisk in almond milk, and set aside to cool completely. Pour cooled mixture into an ice cream machine and freeze according to the manufacturer's directions.

Prepare figs: In a heavy enamel or stainless steel saucepan, heat sugar and water until sugar dissolves. Poach figs in syrup for 4 minutes; remove with a slotted spoon and reserve 12 figs. Purée remaining 4 figs in a blender until smooth; add syrup to thin, if necessary. Strain.

To serve: Coat 4 cold dessert plates with fig purée. Cut off tops of 12 reserved figs and set aside. Arrange 3 figs on each plate and place a small scoop of almond ice cream on each. Place tops of figs on ice cream and decorate plates with grapes.

Makes 4 servings

One way Didier Clément's likes to end a meal: poached figs filled with almond ice cream.

Jean Bardet

L'ESCALOPE DE FOIE GRAS DE CANARD AUX VIEUX VINAIGRE

SCALLOP OF DUCK FOIE GRAS WITH AGED VINEGAR

MIXED VINEGAR:

1½	tablespoons aged Bordeaux wine vinegar
2	teaspoons sherry vinegar
¼	teaspoon unaged wine vinegar

DUCK FOIE GRAS:

¾	to 1 pound raw foie gras, cut into four ½-inch thick slices
	Salt and freshly ground pepper
½	cup flour
1½	tablespoons grapeseed oil, or substitute another mild oil
¼	cup hazelnut oil
1	bunch chives, chopped

Prepare mixed vinegar: In a small bowl, combine the Bordeaux wine vinegar, sherry vinegar, and wine vinegar. Set aside.

Prepare foie gras: Sprinkle foie gras with salt and pepper and dust lightly with flour. In a heavy skillet, heat grapeseed oil. Add foie gras and sauté over medium to high heat for about 3 minutes on each side or until crisp and brown.

Place a slice of foie gras on each of 4 heated serving plates. Baste each piece with 1 tablespoon hazelnut oil and 2 teaspoons mixed vinegar. Sprinkle with chopped chives and serve immediately.

Makes 4 servings

148

Gérard Boyer

ESCALOPE DE TURBOT GRILLEE AUX HUITRES ET AU CAVIAR

GRILLED TURBOT WITH OYSTERS AND CAVIAR

1½	pounds turbot or halibut fillets
18	oysters
⅔	cup Champagne
⅔	cup crème fraîche
½	cup cold unsalted butter, cut into pieces
	Salt and freshly ground pepper
¼	cup peanut oil
	Cayenne pepper
1	ounce Sevruga caviar
1	ounce salmon roe

Rinse fillets and dry well on paper towels. Cut fillets into 6 pieces of equal size. If necessary, flatten fish pieces between sheets of moistened parchment paper so they are of equal thickness.

Preheat grill or broiler.

Shuck oysters into a bowl and strain the liquor into a medium saucepan. Add Champagne. Bring to a boil and cook over high heat for about 15 minutes or until reduced by three quarters. (Note: the sauce will be extremely foamy at first due to the Champagne, so watch carefully.) Whisk in crème fraîche and let sauce return to a boil. Reduce heat to medium and whisk in butter, a few pieces at a time. When all the butter has been incorporated, add oysters and poach them over low heat for 5 minutes. Remove from heat.

Season fish on both sides with salt and pepper; lightly brush with peanut oil. Grill or broil fish, as close to heat as possible, for 2 minutes on each side. Keep warm.

With a slotted spoon, remove oysters from sauce. Reheat sauce gently, whisking constantly, and season to taste with salt, pepper, and cayenne. Ladle sauce onto 6 plates. Place grilled fish on one side of each plate and arrange 3 oysters on the other side. Divide caviar between plates, spooning it between the oysters. Garnish each plate with salmon roe and serve immediately.

Makes 6 servings

Jean Bardet recommends a simple, elegant foie gras preparation.

Facing page: Gérard Boyer's grilled turbot with oysters and caviar should be served warm with cold Champagne.

COUNTRY INNS

OLD-TIME RECIPES AND fresh ingredients: from Périgord to Provence, from Normandy to the Landes, and Auvergne to Gers, for millions of Frenchmen and foreign visitors, real French cooking is not grande cuisine, but fragrant, warming foods like bouillabaisse, boiled pork and cabbage, or a steaming bowlful of tripe. The French are turning back to their regional roots. These dishes are not only nourishing, but are also symbols of the regions that produced them, as evocative of their native soil as landscape, historic buildings, or colorful local customs. A cassoulet, a bourride, or chicken in Bourgueil wine are nothing short of historical monuments that deserve the same protection accorded landmarks.

France is sufficiently rich to number hundreds of men and women, both in modest inns patronized by local farmers or workers and in statelier establishments too, who have become the guardians of a vast and glorious regional heritage that probably numbers ten thousand recipes. Women play a conspicuous and historically important role in preserving these traditions. They learn to cook at their mothers' and grandmothers' knees, then open little restaurants of their own, instead of going on to work in great or well known establishments where for a long time women were not really welcome.

Whether a man or a woman is at the stove, these inns, often (but not always) hidden away in the country, are the best way to discover and grow to love the French heartland. While great restaurants are certainly marvelous, not many provide the warmth and authenticity to be found at Marie-Claude Gracia's, in Poudenas, a village in Gascony with a population of two hundred. Her career began when she and her husband set up a small foie gras canning business, but soon she began thinking of opening a restaurant. She bought an old house in her native village, which she renovated and christened A la Belle Gasconne. Enthusiastic and voluble, Marie-Claude is glad to demonstrate how to cut up a duck, prepare a foie gras, or cook a fish in a casserole with nettles that she has picked along the roadside. Everything at La Belle Gasconne is so pure, so genuine, and so good, from the duck liver terrine to the homemade jams, that you will never want to leave!

A few hundred miles north, in one of the loveliest and best-preserved villages of Normandy, called Beuvron-sur-Auge near Deauville, a fire crackles in the beamed and paneled dining room of Le Pavé d'Auge, situated in the town's sixteenth-century marketplace. Odile Engel, a robust and dynamic woman, is the undisputed queen of Norman cookery, even though she hails from Alsace. So she headed for Normandy, where she fell in love with this village and with all the superb produce available in the region: fish and shellfish that she buys three times a week at the port in Caen, when the little boats come back with their catch of soles, turbots, or John Dory; rabbits, ducks, and pigeons bought at local farms; delicious fresh vegetables and incomparable fresh cream and butter, unlike anything to be found in a supermarket. The Camemberts are rich, unctuous in texture, and delicately flavored. They have become real museum pieces: you can count on your fingers the number of Norman farmers still making the cheese themselves instead of taking their milk to the plant like everyone else. With such singularly fresh ingredients, Odile Engel turns out mussels in cider, rabbit rillettes, huge sautéed sole, turbot in vinegar, tripe, and chicken in cream like you've never tasted. Most people have probably forgotten such flavors even existed!

France produces some excellent meat but it is very hard to find. Nothing can compare with the rib of beef cooked over vine-cuttings served by Jean-Pierre Xiradakis in La Tupina, a genuine country inn in the middle of Old Bordeaux. Despite his Greek patronymic, Jean-Pierre was born in southwest France. He is a champion of local regional products and has created an association of restaurant owners whose cause it is to promote them.

While scouring the environs to find top-quality ingredients, he discovered near Bazas, southeast of Bordeaux, a very old breed of beef. In the sixteenth century, King Henri IV considered their meat to be the best in the realm. For fifty years, the small-scale production of this beef had steadily declined; the breed might well have disappeared had Jean-Pierre, struck by the remarkable quality of the meat it yielded, not banded together with some local restaurateurs to buy large quantities of meat from the remaining cattle ranchers of Bazas. Production took off again as orders began to pour in from all over France. Since Jean-Pierre is also endowed with an expert nose for sniffing out little-known Bordeaux wines and rare Armagnacs, you are

View of the meandering Loire Roiver.

bound to have a memorable time of it when you visit La Tupina.

Périgord, in the Dordogne, was once upon a time reputed for its excellent female cooks. Nowadays, many of that province's restaurant owners serve identical menus, and these same, monotonous specialties (foie gras, preserved goose, truffles, and cèpe mushrooms) may even come from a jar or a can. Such is absolutely not the case at Solange Gardillou's place. About fifteen years ago, she converted a very old mill, Le Moulin du Roc, into a luxurious inn that stands in a village called Champagnac-de-Bélair. One day, her chef simply vanished; Solange, who had no formal training and cooked as her mother had taught her, had no choice but to take over the kitchen herself. She began to look into old recipes she recalled from her youth, like broiled trout stuffed with cèpe mushrooms. She soon began to invent new combinations of her own, with spectacular results. Simplicity, lightness, and harmony are the keynotes of her highly individual style, which produces such small masterpieces as hot foie gras in a cabbage leaf, herb-stuffed legs of guinea hen served with a light-textured sauce of foie gras, or her salmon scallop with leeks. The seventeenth-century mill, its machinery intact, has been lovingly embellished; advance reservations are necessary to obtain one of the eleven delightfully decorated rooms, where you will awaken to the sound of birds singing above the river.

At a wild site on the edge of a river, at the foot of cliffs hollowed out with grottoes that were inhabited in prehistoric times, stands a sixteenth-century manor surrounded by flower beds, vegetable gardens, and orchards. This is La Pescalerie, near the village of Cabrerets, twenty miles from Cahors, in the Quercy region. Two doctors, Roger Belcour and Hélène Com-

bette, have restored it in impeccable taste; to earn back some of their investment, they decided to turn the place into a hotel-restaurant. They furnished the house with fine antiques, lovely fabrics, curios, and modern paintings they had collected. Before opening their ten rooms to guests, the owners tried them, one by one, to make sure that a modern traveler would find in them all that might be needed for comfort and well-being.

Hélène comes from an inn-keeping family, and she has managed to amass scores of savory family recipes that she at first prepared herself. Michel Guérard has since passed on one of his cooks, who is now in charge of the heirloom recipes, though Hélène still keeps an eye on the kitchen. Little do most guests suspect, as they tuck into trout raised in the property's mill stream, the honeyed duck breast, the admirable stuffed cabbage, or the plump and tender farm-raised poultry, the goat cheeses, the succulent desserts, or the wines of Cahors, that the charming, slightly balding gentleman who brings them their food and opens their wine is the head surgeon of the Cahors hospital.

Many French people still buy provisions daily from local greenmarkets.

Facing page: Some markets are open-air; others, like this one in Joigny, are covered. All are central to everyday life in French towns and villages.

Unlike Hélène, Roger Belcour has not abandoned his practice; every morning he heads for the hospital in his aged automobile, which he drives back every evening crammed with provisions purchased at the market or at neighboring farms. When he arrives at La Pescalerie, he pulls on a pair of boots, climbs into a skiff, and hauls in the net that he cast in the river the night before. Afterward, he hurries to the cellar to bring up a few bottles that he will serve with an appreciative flourish to his customers (somewhat surprised to see the "head waiter" dressed in an old sweater instead of a more formal white jacket).

Every restaurant on the Riviera offers "local fish"—they just don't specify which locality the creatures actually come from. In fact, the fish usually arrive fresh or frozen from the Atlantic coast or even from African shores. During the high season, when the demand is greatest, you can count on the fingers of one hand the number of chefs who manage to procure fish actually caught in the waters between Monte Carlo and Saint Tropez. Adrien and Etienne Sordello are members of that small group. More and more

people go to the Restaurant de Bacon in Cap d'Antibes as they would go on a pilgrimage. They are certain to find the freshest, handsomest Mediterranean fish; everyone knows that if only one rock bass remained in the sea, the Sordellos would find it!

If you want to taste a genuine bouillabaisse, visit the Sordellos. Unlike most of their peers, who include only two or three kinds of fish, they make their bouillabaisse with nearly ten varieties, some of which are used just to make the broth. Some people reserve their table a year in advance to be certain they'll have an opportunity to taste this marvelous brew. The restaurant began as a simple wooden hut, and though it has changed somewhat in the last thirty years, it is still a very unpretentious place. If you look up, you may catch a glimpse of Mamma Sordello, who hasn't left her home in fifty years.

Hélène Barale is the queen of Nice's cooks. The restaurant where early in the century her mother prepared Niçois specialties, in addition to selling groceries and coal, has become a kind of municipal monument, filled with hefty farmhouse furniture and kitchen utensils that would

153

make an antique dealer drool. Too weary these days to serve two meals a day, Hélène opens her doors only in the evening, when she offers her customers a single fixed-price meal.

Niçois cooking is one regional cuisine that has withstood the test of time. In the old center of Nice are numerous picturesque eateries that perpetuate this venerable culinary tradition. But Hélène's is a must for the best pissaladières (onion, anchovy, and black olive tarts), soccas (a crêpe made with chickpea flour and olive oil), salade Niçoise (radishes, onions, green peppers, tomatoes, olives, and anchovies), ravioli, and three-meat daubes (stews) that simmer on the stove for three hours and more. Follow that with an extraordinary sweetened Swiss chard tart with apricot jam, coffee, and an old Marc de Provence (grape brandy); if she feels up to it, Hélène may crank up one of her player pianos, and even sing along, just like in her *maman*'s day.

At Chez Fifine in Saint Tropez, if you take care to order in advance, you can indulge in the world's best aioli. About twenty miles away is Bormes-les-Mimosas where the Gedda brothers reign. They are past masters at Provençal cuisine, in their rose-covered restaurant La Tonnelle des Délices.

Edith Remoissent will serve as the grand finale. She lives in a tiny village, Vignoles, just outside Beaune in Burgundy. She is young, attractive, lively, and whimsical. In her vine-covered cottage nestled in the shadow of the church steeple, she has set up large farmhouse tables, benches, a few chairs, and when she reaches her limit of twenty guests, she hangs up a sign that reads "Full." You will be seated amidst jam pots, jars of pickles, huge loaves of bread; beyond the window, you can watch the pet cats and dogs chase chickens in the long grass.

154

Edith learned to cook on her own; indeed, nothing is less like a typical restaurant than Au Petit Truc. No one gets past the door without a reservation, even if the dining room is half empty. And what glorious food! The finest, most authentic, and heart-warming kind of country cooking, rendered with rare imagination and subtlety. Nowhere else will you find an aspic of young rabbit with chervil, an old-fashioned crayfish terrine (a dish that dates from the seventeenth century), a veal terrine with Chablis, or snails with potatoes au gratin to compare with Edith's. Nor so sublime a chocolate tart, made from a jealously guarded secret recipe that Edith swears she will reveal only to the man she marries!

Each day, Hélène Barale offers a single menu of Niçois cooking that reflects the farmer's season and the fisherman's catch.

Facing page: Fishing boats at Cannes, on the French Riviera.

BISTRO CUISINE

THE WORD "BISTRO" IS UNtranslatable, but it is understood the world over. It is an evocative term that summons up images of brownish walls shiny with age, oilcloth on the tables, a zinc-covered bar tended by the owner in shirt-sleeves, who serves up Beaujolais and Côtes-du-Rhône, robust waitresses who joke with the regulars, and the aroma of rabbit stewed with tomatoes and mushrooms or lamb ragoût simmering on the back burner in a kitchen not much bigger than a broom closet.

Along with berets and long loaves of French bread, bistros deserve a place of honor on the French coat of arms. Strangely, the word is not French at all. "Bistro" supposedly dates from the arrival of Russian occupation troops who in 1815 camped out on the Champs-Elysées after Napoleon's defeat at Waterloo. Very thirsty and pressed for time, the czar's soldiers are said to have crowded into the city's cafés crying, "Bystro! bystro!" (that is, "Quick! quick!").

Russian origin or not, the bistro is as much a part of our national heritage as Notre Dame, the Louvre, or the Eiffel Tower. It is a peculiarly Parisian phenomenon, although it has equivalents in all the cities and towns of France. In Lyons, for instance, they are called *bouchons* or *machons*, from the name of the traditional meal based on salted or cured meats (charcuterie) served between 10 and 11 a.m. in these small, always picturesque spots. In Strasbourg, bistros are called "winstubs" (wine bars). They are extremely popular institutions, where a mixed crowd of young and old, rich and less rich, meet in rooms paneled in dark wood, to taste the newest vintage, tuck into hearty dishes cooked by the owner's wife, and laugh and joke in a warm, merry atmosphere.

Traditionally, bistros have been family businesses: Mama or Papa works at the stove, and the staff is solidly entrenched. It is too soon to say that bistros are relics of the past, but it is certain that these little restaurants are seriously threatened by the encroachment of fast-food chains, snack bars, and other forms of eating on the run. Some bistros now have the food they serve delivered from centralized kitchens, where it has been vacuum-packed; although no one wants to admit it, it appears that this system is increasingly widespread. It has become more important than ever to know just where you are eating and how to tell a genuine bistro from the ersatz.

Bistro cuisine is really nothing more or less than the kind of cooking that has always been

At s'Burjerstuewel—a winstub that regular customers call "Chez Yvonne"—in Strasbourg, strangers and friends alike partake of hearty specialties and local wines.

served in French households. It is simple food, truly delicious when lovingly prepared, not steaks and french fries, but slowly simmered dishes like boeuf bourguignon (beef in red wine) or gibelotte de lapin (rabbit stewed in white wine), both of which have a centuries-old tradition behind them. Some are dubbed "specialties of the house" and remain eternally listed on the menu, but most self-respecting bistro chefs pride themselves on varying the offerings daily, according to what is available at the market, seasonal produce, or the mood they are in. When badly done, this kind of cooking (where sauces reign supreme) is a real threat to the digestive tract. But when cooked as it should be, bistro fare can actually be on the light side; in any case, it reawakens childhood memories of the kind of food that Mother (or Grandmother) used to make. While it would be difficult—even if one had the financial means—to lunch or dine daily in a great restaurant, where in the long run the sophisticated food would surely overtax the palate, it is quite possible on the contrary to eat in bistros on a daily basis without ever tiring of the cuisine. And another point in the bistro's favor is that its prices are generally more than reasonable.

One of the most popular is in the heart of historic Paris on the Ile Saint-Louis: Au Gourmet de l'Isle. Owner Jules Bourdeau, who will soon celebrate his eightieth birthday, has for thirty years been serving straightforward, generous fare at unbeatable prices (under ten dollars, all included): beef and lentil salad, fried chitterlings, boiled pork and cabbage, pears in wine, and fruit tarts.

Not far away, at the Pont Marie, Messrs. Griffoul, father and son, post even lower tariffs for the bean soup, pork stew, and chocolate mousse they serve in their hundred-year-old bistro. Near the Place de la Concorde, Lescure is frequented by the U.S. Embassy crowd. In business since 1919, the decor hasn't changed a whit; the unfailingly affable waiters serve an immutable bill of fare: mackerel in white wine, boeuf bourguignon, and leg of lamb with scalloped potatoes are all sure bets.

In the heart of Saint-Germain-des-Prés,

where phony bistros emerge and then sink with appalling speed, Le Petit Saint-Benoît, impervious to fashion, with a decor so authentic that you almost believe it's a stage set, carries on its tradition of vegetable soup, blanquette de veau (veal stew), beef and potato hash, and stewed rhubarb, much to the joy of the writers, painters, and shopkeepers who patronize the place.

In the posh seventh arrondissement, La Fontaine de Mars is another exemplary Parisian bistro of the kind one used to see on any street corner: moleskin banquettes, wooden chairs, yellowish walls, and a bar counter laden with bottles. The tables are placed so close together that one necessarily eavesdrops on the conversation at the next table, and the single fixed meal, priced at around six dollars (including wine), is copious enough to satisfy a stevedore. In the same neighborhood, there is rabbit with polenta, a pot-au-feu (boiled beef), and prune tart on oil-cloth-covered tables at Babkine (Chez Germaine); you'd be hard-pressed to come up with better versions of these dishes at home. Au Pied de Fouet, too, has remained virtually unchanged since the days when it was a favorite haunt with coachmen employed in the elegant Faubourg Saint-Germain. Nobel-prize-winning writer André Gide, who lived close by, regularly lunched there in the 1950s. You may even find yourself seated at his usual table when you start in on your chitterlings or your floating island with caramel, which won't take you over the eight- or nine-dollar mark.

In Montmartre, Le Petit Marguery offers simple but charming fare. Le Bateau Lavoir is set in the famous studio where early in the century Picasso, Utrillo, and other artists ate cheaply before they became rich and famous.

Not all bistros are inexpensive eateries. There are classes, hierarchies: above the "little bistros" are the big ones. Not big in terms of size, but because of their reputation for fine food and the far more elegant style of their clientele.

For three or four decades, Allard, situated on the Left Bank, was one of the undisputed champions of the upscale bistro category, where over the years so many celebrities sat down to dine. Sad to say, I'm not sure that it can still be recommended, for Fernande Allard has decided to retire from the kitchen. Only time will reveal if

With typical bistro warmth, Bar de la Nouvelle invites customers.

her successor is worthy of the fantastic reputation of this bistro. Benoît, on the other hand, is as reliable as when it opened for business in 1912. The founder's grandson, Michel, has taken great care to preserve the room's original decor as well as the traditional offerings that have made this bistro famous. These include hot sausage and the wonderful braised beef.

On the outskirts of the old Marais quarter, L'Ambassade d'Auvergne is not, strictly speaking, a Parisian bistro. The two dining rooms set in an old private house give the impression of a little village restaurant in Auvergne, what with the beams, the fat hams hanging from the ceiling, and the huge farmhouse table where single diners may sit with their fellow man. You won't regret your choice when you taste the best raw ham in Paris and other filling and savory dishes like boudin (blood sausage) with chestnuts, Auvergne-style boiled meats, lentil cassoulet, or stuffed cabbage. The prices are higher than in a neighborhood bistro, but far lower than those in a great restaurant. The food is so good and the welcome so warm that most guests feel they've got a tremendous bargain.

The reigning monarch of top-of-the-line Parisian bistros remains L'Ami Louis. The owner's real name isn't Louis but Antoine. He was born in a working-class quarter of Paris almost ninety years ago and trained as a cook in Switzerland, but he speaks with a Burgundy accent and has a weakness for southwestern cuisine. For nearly fifty years, with unexampled vigilance, Monsieur Magnin has kept his premises in a state of studied dilapidation and high-toned indigence that deserves to be preserved in a museum of folklore. Until very recently, the bistro's windows still showed traces of the blue paint that was obligatory during World War II to filter bright light. Magnin finally decided to scrape it off, but the rest of the place is (if we may use the expression) intact: peeling paint, wooden tables, rickety chairs, indescribable toilets, and dim lighting. The kitchen, likewise, is kept in deliberate disorder. There the youthful old chef, who sometimes breaks out in epic rages but who may also prove a charming host, prepares heavenly food: fresh foie gras, ham from the Landes, ribs of beef, cèpe mushrooms, tender leg of lamb with scrumptious crusty skin—

159

Especially when the Beaujolais Nouveau arrives, Bar de la Nouvelle does a brisk business.

all are wonderfully good, and the portions are fit for giants. The smallest plate holds enough food for two or three hungry people. If he's asked in a way he finds tactful, the waiter may consent to divide the servings. Leftovers go to feed the neighborhood stray dog, Magnin's pet (!) charity. Thus, when you pay the tab, which will come to forty or so dollars a head, you can rest assured that you are contributing to an excellent cause.

Clockwise from top left, this page: Willi's, a wine bar in Paris, offers over one hundred wines by the glass and sturdy English food. The fifty-year-old L'Ami Louis is perhaps the top bistro in Paris for traditional cooking. Jacques Melac's pub in Paris offers daily specials, wines by the glass, and good company.

Facing page: Bridge in Joigny.

THE PLEASURES OF FRENCH WINE

Chapter

7

FRANCE NUMBERS 875,000 winegrowers, each producing a wine that is perceptibly different from his neighbors. In the Bordeaux region alone there are more than two thousand châteaux, with each property having its own name—there is only one Château Mouton-Rothschild, for example. But in Burgundy there are 114 different appellations, and each may comprise hundreds, indeed thousands, of wines that are utterly dissimilar. When you see the name Clos de Vougeot on a wine list, you know that it is one of Burgundy's most prestigious growths; but this hundred-some acre parcel of land belongs to seventy owners who all make Clos de Vougeot, and if you don't know the names of those who make it well, you risk disappointment. The same principle applies in Chablis, where three hundred proprietors share the appellation. And so it goes, from Chambertin to Corton-Charlemagne.

Because of the great diversity of French wine, the sommelier's knowledge and taste take years to perfect, and he or she should be regarded with respect and confidence. Traditionally, wine stewards themselves adopted solemn attitudes, carrying out their office with the pomp and majesty conferred by long tradition. At one great restaurant in Burgundy, the wine basket was carried into the dining room as if it were the Sacrament. When, after swirling the wine in a glass and breathing in the bouquet with closed eyes, the sommelier at last took a sip of the wine and rolled it on his tongue, the whole dining room would wait, breathless. Conscious of the effect he was creating, he would pause for a moment before handing down his verdict (always favorable, incidentally), signaled by a slow and dignified nod.

Fifteen years ago, that kind of scene was still common. But a new wave of young sommeliers has begun to change the code. Wine education has become much broader and much more technically oriented than in the past. Young wine stewards no longer stage liturgies, but instead try to show customers how to take advantage of their expertise. The ritual of serving wine is simpler now, with sommeliers aiming to intensify customers' pleasure.

The present generation must be more dynamic than their predecessors. In the days when a restaurant gauged the quality of its wine list by the number of famous names it could boast, sommeliers knew they couldn't go wrong recommending a Latour, an Yquem, or a Romanée-Conti. Today, a wine list on which famous

Tradition dictates that guests at Tour d'Argent descend to the famous wine cellar for an after-dinner Cognac or Armagnac.

growths are listed beside lesser-known but choice bottles selected for their quality and their personality is considered more impressive, so sommeliers need a broader range of expertise. Many make frequent trips to the wine regions and attend comparative wine tastings.

This new breed is an elite, of course, and the stars are Marcel Périnet (Georges Blanc, in Vonnas), George Pertuiset (Lameloise, in Chagny), Werner Heil (Gerard Boyer, in Reims), Jean-Claude Jambon (Faugeron, in Paris), Marc Brockart (Apicius, in Paris), Antoine Hernandez (Robuchon, in Paris), Jean-Claude Maître (Le Crillon, Paris), Jean-Pierre Rous (Le Royal-Gray, Cannes), Jean Jacques (Bardet, in Châteauroux), Jacques Mélac (42 rue Leon Frot, Paris), Jean-Luc Pouteau (Le Pavillon de l'Elysée, Paris). The latter won the title of "World's Best Sommelier" in Brussels. There are others, of course, too numerous to name.

Wine madness has seized a growing number of chefs and restaurateurs. Many of them play the role of sommelier themselves, purchasing their own wine at the vineyards, taking courses in oenology, participating in blind tastings. Some of them have become leading wine experts. Although some restaurants offer less than the best vintages of the best wines, all the fine establishments in this book, and most other restaurants, regard wine as an object of fervent interest. A case in point was the late, much lamented Jean Troisgros, who was pretty nearly unbeatable in blind tastings; other illustrious ones are Alain Chapel, Jacques Pic, Pierre Laporte, Michel Guérard, Marc Meneau, Jean-Claude Vrinat, Alain Dutournier, Guy Savoy, Michel Oliver, Alain Senderens, Lucien Vanel, Michel Trama, Christian Clément, Jean-Marie Amat, Pierre Menneveau (at Rôtisserie du Chambertin, in Gevrey-Chambertin), and dozens of others. Women are not yet very numerous, but often prove to have exceptional flair, as in the cases of Jacqueline Lorain (in Joigny), Sophie Bardet (in Châteauroux), Madame Barrat (Le Lion d'Or, in Romorantin), or Maryse Allarousse (Le Panorama, in Dardilly, near Lyon), who even captured the title "Best Sommelière in France."

Of all the pleasures of the table, wine arouses the most curiosity. It has its own special lore, not necessarily rational, which has been handed down from generation to generation. But because gastronomy, including the choice of a wine, is ideally an art of nuance, only your own experience and pleasure should determine your likes and dislikes. All of the once-inviolable laws have in fact been questioned during the past twenty years, and as many have been found wrong-headed as have been justified. People are more open-minded, trying unexpected combinations of wine and food. Some, like Sophie Bardet or Alain Senderens, have gone so far as to compose meals around wines, instead of vice versa.

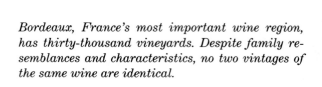

Bordeaux, France's most important wine region, has thirty-thousand vineyards. Despite family resemblances and characteristics, no two vintages of the same wine are identical.

164

It is an interesting experiment to try yourself; if you have some favorite wines, consider asking the restaurant owner in advance to compose a meal around them. It may well be one of the greatest gustatory pleasures of your life.

Even without going quite so far, it is worthwhile to keep some unconventional but exciting possibilities in mind. Here are a few ideas.

1. It is not true that mixing red and white wines brings on headaches; headaches result from overindulgence. A thoughtful combination of white and red wines can create harmonies and contrasts that you would miss if you limited yourself to a single wine.

2. It is not necessarily true that an older wine should be decanted. Prolonged contact with air often "kills" the wine. In a test with two bottles of Lafite-Rothschild 1870, one was opened two hours before the meal and decanted into a carafe; it lost a great deal of its aroma. The second bottle, uncorked at the last moment, had all its bouquet intact. However, a young or slightly hard red wine may gain from being decanted, for the

contact with oxygen will soften it a bit.

3. The practice of bringing red wine to room temperature was justified when houses were chilly and the wine was brought directly from the cellar where the temperature hovered around 53° F. Today, apartments are generally well heated, and it is absurd to bring a Bordeaux or Burgundy to a room temperature of 68° F because the wine becomes heavy and unpleasant to drink. To appreciate a good red wine, it should not be warmer than about 63° F for a Bordeaux, 58° F for a red Burgundy. But a too-low temperature can kill some wines. A Beaujolais served in an ice-bucket will not release its bouquet, and a white Burgundy or Côtes-du-Rhône will be far better at 54° F than if served icy cold. An Alsatian wine, or a Loire Valley white will be perfect at about 51° F. And as a general rule, a young, or "hard," red wine will improve if served cold, for its fruit will be more apparent.

4. It is a mistake to serve too many great wines at one meal. A great opera production rarely has a half-dozen divas! One or two are more than sufficient: that way, instead of competing they can complement each other.

5. Memorable meals can center around modest wines, as long as they have been chosen with care. There are innumerable appealing little wines like Saint-Véran (Burgundy), Chinon (Loire), Cornas (Côtes-du-Rhône), Bandol (Provence), Bergerac (southwest), and many others that can harmonize nicely.

Here are some suggestions for marrying wines with food.

Foie gras: Sauternes is fine, but other white wines would go well too, like a Meursault or Montrachet from Burgundy, an Alsatian Tokay or Gewürtztraminer, a Savennières from the Loire, or a Condrieu, Hermitage, or Château-

Regardless of the color of the skin, the juice of red wine grapes is colorless. The final red color comes from fermenting the juice with the skins and pips, which are eventually removed.

neuf-du-Pape from the Côtes-du-Rhône; or you could try a Beaumes-de-Venise from that area, which is a bit like Sauternes, only less sweet. Certain red wines are agreeable accompaniments too: rustic wines like Cahors and Bergerac, or even a Bordeaux Cru Bourgeois.

If you have it at the end of the meal, just before the cheese, foie gras pairs off beautifully with an old red or white port, or even a Sherry that you can continue to drink with some Roquefort cheese.

Oysters and Shellfish: Muscadet is often recommended, and a good one such as Metaireau's is fine. But Muscadet is often too acid, so you might prefer a dry white Graves, a Sancerre, a Chablis, or even a big, tasty Bourgogne like Corton-Charlemagne. Don't neglect young reds that may be drunk chilled, like Chinon, Bandol, Coteaux d'Aix-en-Provence, or an Alsatian Pinot Noir. They all go well with the iodine flavor of oysters.

Crustaceans: With cold lobster, crab, or prawns choose a dry white wine with some fruitiness, like a Sancerre, a Quincy, a Saint Pour-çain, or a Riesling. If they are served hot, crustaceans marry well with nobler, softer wines: Pouilly-Fuissé, Meursault, Puligny-Montrachet (all Burgundies), Coulée de Serrant (Anjou), Hermitage, Saint-Joseph, or Condrieu (Côtes-du-Rhône).

Fish: With fish in a butter sauce, try white wines from the Loire (Saumur, Sancerre, Pouilly-Fumé). With red wine sauces, drink the same red wine, or else a fat white wine from Burgundy or the Côtes-du-Rhône, which will contrast with the sauce, yet not overwhelm it. If you are having smoked salmon or caviar, red wine is disastrous. But with fresh grilled salmon accompanied by a sauce Béarnaise, or even with a grilled sole, a cool red wine (Bordeaux, Loire, Beaujolais, or Bouzy from Champagne) would be just the ticket. With little fried fish, Muscat d'Alsace is lovely; with bouillabaisse, try a white wine from Provence, a Cassis, for example.

Lamb: With milk-fed lamb, the best choice would be a medium-bodied red (Pauillac, Saint-Estèphe, Saint-Julien). With a leg or saddle of lamb, a great Bordeaux or a good Provençal

166

The French grape harvest begins in late September or early October.

wine (Côtes d'Aix, Bandol). With lamb or mutton in a sauce, choose a red from the Loire (Saumur-Champigny, Bourgueil), a Côtes-du-Rhône (Gigondas), or a wine from Languedoc (Fitou, Corbières).

Beef: If it's a grilled cut, any simple red wine will do (Beaujolais, Languedoc, Côtes-du-Rhône Villages, a modest Bordeaux). If the meat is of exceptional quality, pick something a cut above. With an excellent beef rib grilled over vine cuttings the way they do in Bordeaux, there's no reason not to select a superb Médoc, or even a prestigious Pomerol. In Normandy, I once was served a glass of Calvados with my beef. After a moment of hesitation, I took a sip: fantastic. Pot-au-feu takes a rustic red wine (Morgon, Cahors, Côtes de Buzet, Bergerac, Chinon), and with boeuf bourguignon, choose a relatively simple Burgundy, like a Rully, a Passe-tout-grain, or a Mercurey.

Pork: With charcuterie, a cool Gamay, a Beaujolais, or else a dry white Vouvray. Cooked, pork is generally a rich or even fatty meat, and requires a fresh young red, served cool, like a

Château Monbazillac is the estate of Bergerac's most well known wine, a rich, white dessert wine resembling Sauternes.

Beaujolais, Pinot Noir d'Alsace, a Cahors, or a Bergerac. These same wines are fine with choucroute (sauerkraut), which need not always be accompanied by a white Alsatian wine.

Chicken: There's nothing better with broiled chicken than a young red wine from the Côtes de Beaune (Savigny, Blagny), the Médoc, or the Loire (Champigny, Bourgueil). If the chicken is prepared in a cream sauce, try a white Burgundy (Meursault) or a light red, say a Beaujolais.

The individuality of a wine starts with the grapes, the soil, and the climate.

Duck: This fowl calls for sturdy, structured wines: a great Medoc, a Pomerol, a Hermitage; but don't overlook less prestigious wines like Cahors, Madiran, or a Saint-Joseph from the Côtes-du-Rhône.

Game: White-fleshed game (pheasant or partridge) goes very well with light red Burgundies (Chambolle-Musigny, Clos de Vougeot), but do try a roast young partridge with a white Burgundy such as Bâtard-Montrachet; you are sure to be agreeably surprised. Dark-fleshed game (venison, hare, boar) calls for rich and powerful red wines: Gevrey-Chambertin, Pommard (Burgundies), Châteauneuf-du-Pape, Côte Rôtie, Hermitage (Côtes-du-Rhône), or a great Pomerol. But certain sweet white wines (Sauternes, Anjou), or an old Tokay d'Alsace, or even a great old white Burgundy (Corton-Charlemagne) can complement the rich taste of game in sauce.

Cheeses: Red wines are not the only ones that should be drunk with a Brie, Roquefort, or farm-cured Camembert. A strong cheese kills a great wine, so the best choice is a robust, tannic red wine, like red Sancerre, Côtes-du-Rhône Villages, Bergerac, Cahors, or Madiran. Certain white wines make good partners for some cheeses, for example Sauternes with Roquefort, white Hermitage with Saint-Nectaire, Riesling with Munster or Livarot, wines from Savoie with Gruyère or Tomme, and Sancerre with goat cheeses.

Desserts: It is notoriously difficult to choose a wine to end the meal, since desserts containing alcohol or based on fruit do not go well with wine. In a pinch, you can serve a light red or white (Anjou, Saumur, Bourgueil, Sancerre) with a fruit tart, and with pastries, a dry white Graves. A Muscat de Beaumes-de-Venise or an old white Banyuls (a naturally sweet wine from the Eastern Pyrénées, aged in barrels set out in the sun) are marvelous with chocolate desserts. Another unusual but delicious match is medium-dry Sherry with fruit sherbets. Another quite suitable solution is to end the meal with the white or red wine that accompanied the preceding course.

And why not try Champagne? Sixty percent of the Champagne consumed in France is drunk with dessert. Try a pink Champagne. Its solid structure goes admirably with the sweet flavors of desserts.

APPENDIXES

I BORDEAUX AND BURGUNDY VINTAGES

Just like a living being, wine evolves, improves, or deteriorates with time. As it ages, a mediocre vintage may turn out to be a winner. Unfortunately, the reverse is also true. What follows is an overview of the last several vintages in Bordeaux and Burgundy.

EXCEPTIONAL YEAR	*****
VERY GREAT YEAR	****
GREAT YEAR	***
GOOD YEAR	**
MEDIOCRE YEAR	*
POOR YEAR	-

BORDEAUX

Year		Rating	Year		Rating
1984	Reds	*	1978	Reds	****
	Whites	**		Whites	-
1983	Reds	****	1977	Reds	-
	Whites	***		Whites	-
1982	Reds	*****	1976	Reds	**
	Whites	**		Whites	**
1981	Reds	****	1975	Reds	*
	Whites	**		Whites	***
1980	Reds	**	1970	Reds	****
	Whites	*		Whites	***
1979	Reds	***			
	Whites	*			

BURGUNDIES

Year		Rating	Year		Rating
1984	Reds	*	1978	Reds	****
	Whites	**		Whites	*
1983	Reds	**	1976	Reds	****
	Whites	***		Whites	****
1982	Reds	**			
	Whites	****			
1981	Reds	*			
	Whites	*			
1980	Reds	-			
	Whites	-			
1979	Reds	**			
	Whites	***			

The most famous sparkling wines in the world are produced in northeastern France, near Reims, where the kings of France were once crowned. The process that cultivates the bubbles in fine Champagne takes six or seven years, during which time a bottle may be handled two hundred times.

II THE GREAT WINES OF BORDEAUX

Since 1855 the red wine of Bordeaux has been divided into five categories of "growths." Recently, Gault-Millau magazine conducted a survey in which three hundred specialists (oenologists, brokers, sommeliers, wine merchants) were questioned in an attempt to establish a hierarchy of the best red Bordeaux. What follows are lists of our specialists' favorites, in the order of preference on a scale of 1 to 100.

Premièrs Crus (First growths)	
Latour	98
Margaux	90
Haut-Brion	90
Mouton-Rothschild	88
Lafite-Rothschild	85

Deuxièmes Crus (Second growths)	
Ducru-Beaucaillou	96
Pichon-Longueville, Comtesse de Lalande	96
Léoville-Las Cases	95
Cos d'Estournel	89
Gruaud-Larose	71

Troisièmes Crus (Third growths)	
Palmer	97
Giscours	95
La Lagune	94
Calon-Ségur	89

Quatrièmes Crus (Fourth growths)	
Prieuré-Lichine	91
Talbot	89
Duhart-Milon-Rothschild	88
Beychevelle	84

Cinquièmes Crus (Fifth growths)	
Lynch-Bages	100
Grand-Puy-Lacoste	100
Haut-Batailley	100
Dauzac	98
Cantemerle	96
Clerc-Milon	96
Pontet-Canet	94
Mouton-Baronne-Philippe	93
Batailley	91

Although they are less renowned, the Cru Bourgeois of the Médoc are very fashionable right now; they are excellent buys. Our jury of specialists singled out the following wines as particularly worthy of note:

Chasse-Spleen, Gloria, de Pez, Sociando-Mallet, Phelan-Ségur, Meyney, Poujeaux-Theil, Haut-Marbuzet, Siran, Bel-Air-Marquis d'Aligre, Lanessan.

The official classification of 1855 included only one wine from the Graves region: Haut-Brion. This state of affairs ought to be righted; here are some of today's best wines from Graves:

La Mission-Haut-Brion, Domaine de Chevalier, Haut-Bailly, Pape-Clément, Smith-Haut-Lafitte, Fieuzal, Carbonnieux, Bouscaut, Olivier.

The red wines of Pomerol are not subject to any classification, although they are among the best wines of Bordeaux. They often command higher prices than the most well known Médocs ($2,000 at the Hôtel Ritz for a bottle of Petrus 1947). Herewith, a short list of the "stars" of Pomerol in the order of my personal preference:

Petrus, Trotanoy, L'Evangile, Lafleur-Petrus, La Conseillante, Petit-Village, Latour-Pomerol, Vieux-Château-Certan, Certan de May, Lagrange, Nenin, Gazin, L'Eglise, L'Eglise-Clinet, Clos René, La Pointe, Le Bon Pasteur, Beauregard.

The red wines of Saint-Emilion are innumerable and have their own classification system. The following are some of the most highly regarded:

Cheval Blanc, Figeac, Ausone, L'Angélus, La Gaffelière, Pavie, Balestard-la-Tonnelle, Corbin-Michotte, Grand-Barrail-Lamarzelle-Figeac, Grand-Mayne, Grand-Corbin, La Dominique, Saint-Georges, Soutard, Grâce-Dieu.

And finally, Sauternes, considered to be the best sweet white wines on earth:

d'Yquem, Suduiraut, Coutet, Climens, Guiraud, Lafaurie-Peyraguey, Rieussec, Filhot, de Malle, de Rayne-Vigneau, Haut-Peyraguey, La Tour-Blanche, Gilette.

III RESTAURANT ADDRESSES

PARIS

1st arrondissement

Le Carré des Feuillants
14 rue de Castiglione
42.96.67.92.
Service until 10:30 pm.
Closed Saturday and Sunday.
Card: V.

Le Grand Véfour
17 rue de Beaujolais
42.96.56.27.
Service until 10:15 pm.
Closed Saturday,
Sunday; August.
Cards: V, AE, DC.

Lescure
7 rue de Mondovi
42.60.18.91.
Service until 10 pm.
Closed Saturday
evening and Sunday.

Vendôme (Hôtel Ritz)
15 place Vendôme
42.60.38.30.
Open daily.
Cards: V, AE, DC, EC.

3rd arrondissement

L'Ambassade d'Auvergne
22 rue du Grenier-
Saint-Lazare
42.72.31.22.
Service until 1 am.
Closed Sunday.
Cards: V.

L'Ami Louis
32 rue du Vertbois
48.87.77.48.
Service until 10:30 pm.
Closed Monday, Tuesday;
July 1–September 30.
Cards: V, AE, DC.

4th arrondissement

Benoît
20 rue Saint-Martin
42.72.25.76.
Service until 10 pm.
Closed Saturday,
Sunday; August.

Au Gourmet de l'Isle
42 rue Saint-Louis-en-l'Ile
43.26.79.27.
Service until 9:30 pm.
Closed Monday, Thursday;
July 25–September 1.

Au Pont Marie
7 quai de Bourbon
43.54.79.62.
Service until 10 pm.
Closed Saturday and Sunday.

5th arrondissement

La Tour d'Argent
15–17 quai de la Tournelle
43.54.23.31.
Service until 10 pm.
Closed Monday.
Cards: V, AE, DC.

6th arrondissement

Allard
41 rue Saint-André-dés-Arts
43.26.48.23.
Service until 10:30 pm.
Closed Saturday,
Sunday; August.
Cards: V, DC.

Jacques Cagna
14 rue des
Grands Augustins
43.26.49.39.
Service until 10:30 pm.
Closed Saturday, Sunday;
December 24–
January 2; August.
Cards: V, AE, DC.

Lapérouse
51 quai des
Grands Augustins
43.26.68.04.
Service until 11 pm.
Closed Saturday lunch,
Sunday.
Cards: V, AE, DC, EC.

Le Petit Saint-Benoît
4 rue Saint-Benoît
42.60.27.92.
Service until 10 pm.
Closed Saturday and Sunday.

7th arrondissement

Babkine (Chez Germaine)
30 rue Pierre-Leroux
42.73.28.34.
Service until 9 pm.
Closed Saturday evening,
Sunday; August.

Le Bourdonnais
113 ave. de la Bourdonnais
47.05.47.96.
Service until 11 pm.
Closed Sunday and Monday.
Cards: V, AE, DC.

Le Divellec
107 rue de l'Université
45.51.91.96.
Service until 10 pm.
Closed Sunday, Monday;
December 24–January 2;
August 2–September 2.
Cards: V, AE, DC.

La Fontaine de Mars
129 rue Saint-Dominique
47.05.46.44.
Service until 9:15 pm.
Closed Saturday evening
and Sunday.

Au Pied de Fouet
45 rue de Babylone
47.05.12.27.
Service until 9 pm.
Closed Saturday evening
and Sunday.

Jules Verne
Eiffel Tower (2nd floor)
45.55.61.44.
Service until 10:30 pm.
Open daily.
Cards: V, AE.

8th arrondissement

Les Ambassadeurs
(Hôtel de Crillon)
10 place de la Concorde
42.65.24.24.
Service until 10:30 pm.
Open daily.
Cards: V, AE, DC.

Laurent
41 ave. Gabriel
47.23.79.18.
Service until 11 pm.
Closed Saturday lunch,
Sunday.
Cards: AE, DC.

Lucas-Carton
9 place de la Madeleine
42.65.22.90.
Service until 10:30 pm.
Closed Saturday, Sunday;
August 2–22.
Card: V.

Maxim's
3 rue Royale
42.65.27.94.
Service until 1 am.
Closed Sunday.
Cards: V, AE, DC.

Pavillon de l'Elysée
10 Champs-Elysées
42.65.85.10.
Service until 11 pm.
Closed Saturday, Sunday;
August 2–31.
Cards: V, AE, DC.

Taillevent
15 rue Lamennais
45.63.39.94.
Service until 10:30 pm.
Closed Saturday, Sunday;
July 26–August 25.

15th arrondissement

Olympe
8 rue Nicolas-Charlet
47.34.86.08.
Service until 12 midnight.
Closed Monday; lunch
(except Thursday);
August 1–22.
Cards: V, AE, DC.

16th arrondissement

Robuchon
32 rue de Longchamp
47.27.12.27.
Service until 10:15 pm.
Closed Saturday, Sunday;
June 30–July 27.
Cards: V, AE, DC.

Guy Savoy
28 rue Duret
45.00.17.67.
Service until 10:30 pm.
Closed Saturday, Sunday.
Card: V.

17th arrondissement

Le Manoir de Paris
6 rue Pierre Demours
45.72.25.25.
Service until 10:30 pm.
Closed Saturday, Sunday;
July 5–August 4.
Cards: V, AE, DC.

Michel Rostang
20 rue Rennequin
47.63.40.77.
Service until 10:15 pm.
Closed Saturday (except
lunch May–September),
Sunday; July 26–August 26.
Card: V.

18th arrondissement

Le Bateau Lavoir
8 rue Garreau
46.06.02.00.
Service until 10 pm.
Open daily.

Le Petit Marguery
8 rue Aristide Bruant
42.64.95.81.
Service until 9:30 pm.
Closed Sunday, Monday; September.

Outside Paris

La Vieille Fontaine
8 ave. Gréty
49.62.01.78.
Service until 10 pm.
Closed Sunday, Monday;
August.
Cards: V, AE, DC.

THE PROVINCES

ALSACE

Auberge de l'Ill
Rue de Collonges
Illhaeusern
68150 Ribeauvillé
89.71.83.23.
Service until 9 pm.
Closed Monday
(evening only in summer),
Tuesday; 1st week of July.
Cards: AE, DC.

Le Crocodile
10 rue de l'Outre
67000 Strasbourg
88.32.13.02.
Service until 10 pm.
Closed Sunday, Monday;
July 8–August 4.
Cards: AE, DC.

BURGUNDY

Georges Blanc
(La mère Blanc)
01540 Vonnas
74.50.00.10.
Service until 9:30 pm.
Cards: V, AE, DC.

La Côte d'Or
2 rue d'Argentine
21210 Saulieu
80.64.07.66.
Service until 10 pm.
Closed Tuesday;
Wednesday lunch
(November 1–March 31,
exc. holidays).
Cards: V, AE, DC.

La Côte Saint-Jacques
14 Faubourg de Paris
89300 Joigny
86.62.09.70.
Service until 9:30 pm.
Cards: V, AE, DC.

L'Espérance
Saint-Père-sous-Vézelay
89450 Vézelay
86.33.20.45.
Service until 9:30 pm.
Closed Tuesday,
Wednesday lunch.
Cards: V, AE.

Lameloise
36 place d'Armes
71150 Chagny
85.87.08.85.
Service until 9:30 pm.
Closed Wednesday evening,
Thursday lunch.
Card: V.

Au Petit Truc
Place de l'Eglise
21200 Beaune
80.22.01.76.
Service until 9 pm.
Closed Monday, Tuesday;
August 3–21.

BRITTANY, NORMANDY

Le Bretagne
13 rue Saint-Michel
56230 Questembert
97.26.11.12.
Service until 9:30 pm.
Closed Sunday evening
(exc. July, August).
Cards: V, AE, DC.

Château de Locguénolé
Route de Port-Louis
56700 Hennebont
97.76.29.04.
Service until 9:30 pm.
Cards: V, AE, DC, EC.

Le Pavé d'Auge
Place du Village
14430 Dozulé
31.79.26.71.
Service until 9 pm.
Closed Tuesday and
Wednesday evenings.
Cards: V, AE.

Restaurant de Bricourt
1 rue Duguesclin
35260 Cancale
99.89.64.76.
Service until 9:30 pm.
Closed Tuesday, Wednesday.
Cards: V, EC.

CHAMPAGNE AND THE NORD

Boyer (Château des Crayères)
64 blvd. Henry-Vasnier
51100 Reims
26.82.80.80.
Service until 9:30 pm.
Closed Monday,
Tuesday lunch.
Cards: V, AE, DC, EC.

Le Flambard
79 rue d'Angleterre
59000 Lille
20.51.00.06.
Service until 9:30 pm.
Closed Sunday evening,
Tuesday; August.
Cards: AE, DC.

RIVIERA

Barale
39 rue Beaumont
06000 Nice
Service until 9 pm.
Closed Saturday.
Dinner only.

Chantecler (Hôtel Negresco)
37 Promenade des Anglais
06000 Nice
93.88.39.51.
Open daily.
Service until 10:30 pm.
Cards: V, AE, DC, EC.

Chez Fifine
5 rue Cépoun-San-Martin
83990 Saint Tropez
94.97.03.90.
Closed Monday; off-
season.

Dominique Le Stanc
18 blvd. des Moulins
Monte Carlo
93.50.63.37.
Service until 10 pm.
Closed Sunday, Monday.
Cards: V, AE, DC.

Le Moulin de Mougins
424 chemin du Moulin
Quartier Notre-Dame-de-Vie
06250 Mougins
93.75.78.24.
Service until 10:30 pm.
Closed Monday,
Thursday; lunch.
Cards: V, AE, DC.

L'Oasis
Rue Jean-Honoré-Carle
06210 Mandelieu
93.49.95.52.
Service until 9:30 pm.
Closed Monday evening,
Tuesday.

La Palme d'Or
(Hôtel Martinez)
73 blvd. de la Croisette
06400 Cannes
93.84.10.24.
Service until 11 pm.
Cards: VC, AE, DC, EC.

Restaurant de Bacon
Blvd. de Bacon
06600 Cap d'Antibes
93.61.77.70.
Service until 10 pm.
Closed Sunday evening,
Monday; November 15–
February 1.
Cards: AE, DC.

Le Royal-Gray
(Hôtel Gray d'Albion)
6 rue des Etats-Unis
06400 Cannes
93.48.54.54.
Service until 10 pm.
Closed Sunday evening;
Monday off-season.
Cards: V, AE, DC.

La Terrasse (Hôtel Juana)
Ave. Georges-Gallice
06160 Juan-les-Pins
93.61.20.37.
Service until 10 pm.
Dinner only (July 1–
August 31).
Closed October 20–March 20.

172

La Tonnelle des Délices
Place Gambetta
83230 Bormes-les-Mimosas
94.71.34.84.
Service until 10 pm.
Closed October 1–March 31.

PROVENCE

L'Oustau de Baumanière
Au Val d'Enfer
13520 Maussane-les-Alpilles
90.97.33.07.
Service until 9:45 pm.
Closed Wednesday, Thursday
lunch.
Cards: V, AE, DC, EC.

LYONS AND THE RHÔNE VALLEY

Paul Bocuse
50 quai de la Plage
69660 Collonges-
au-Mont-d'Or
78.22.01.40.
Service until 9:30 pm.
Cards: V, AE, DC.

Alain Chapel
RN 83
01390 Saint-André-de-Corcy
79.91.82.02.
Service until 10 pm.
Cards: AE, DC.

Pierre Gagnaire
3 rue Georges-Teissier
42000 Saint-Etienne
77.37.57.93.
Service until 9:30 pm.
Closed Sunday, Monday;
August 9–September 9.
Cards: V, AE, DC.

Léon de Lyon
1 rue Pleney
(1st arrondissement)
69000 Lyon
78.28.11.23.
Service until 10 pm.
Closed Monday lunch, Sunday.
Card: V.

Pic
285 ave. Victor-Hugo
26000 Valence
75.44.15.32.
Service until 9:30 pm.
Closed Sunday evening,
Wednesday; August.
Cards: AE, DC.

La Tour Rose
16 rue du Boeuf (5th)
69000 Lyon
78.37.25.90.
Closed Sunday.
Cards: V, AE, DC, EC.

Troisgros
Place de la Gare
42300 Roanne
77.71.66.97.
Service until 9:30 pm.
Closed Tuesday,
Wednesday lunch; August.
Cards: V, AE, DC.

MASSIF CENTRAL

Lou Mazuc
12210 Laguiole
65.44.32.24.
Service until 9 pm.
Closed Sunday evening;
Monday (exc. July–August).
Card: AE.

LOIRE REGION

Jean Bardet
1 rue J.-J. Rousseau
36000 Châteauroux
54.34.82.69.
Service until 9:30 pm.
Closed Sunday evening;
Monday.
Cards: V, AE, DC, EC.

Le Lion d'Or
69 rue Georges-Clemenceau
41200 Romorantin
54.76.00.28.
Service until 9 pm.
Cards: V, AE, DC, EC.

Le Relais
1 ave. de Chambord
41250 Bracieux
54.46.41.22.
Service until 9 pm.
Closed Tuesday evening,
Wednesday.
Cards: V, AE, DC.

PÉRIGORD-QUERCY

Le Moulin du Roc
24530 Champagnac-de-Bélair
53.54.80.36.
Service until 9:30 pm.
Closed Tuesday,
Wednesday evening.
Cards: V, AE, DC, EC.

La Pescalerie
46330 Cabrerets
65.31.22.55.
Service until 9 pm.
Closed November 1–April 1.
Cards: V, AE, DC.

SOUTHWEST

L'Aubergade
52 rue Royale
47270 Puymirol
53.95.31.46.
Service until 9:30 pm.
Closed Monday (exc. July–
August and holidays).
Cards: V, AE.

A la Belle Gasconne
47170 Mézin
53.65.71.58.
Service until 9:30 pm.
Closed Sunday evening,
Monday; January 16–
February 10, November 1–15.
Cards: V, AE, DC.

Clavel
44 rue Charles-Domercq
33000 Bordeaux
56.92.91.52.
Service until 9:30 pm.
Closed Sunday, Monday;
July 15–31; February
school holidays.
Cards: AE, DC, V.

Dubern
42 allées de Tourny
33000 Bordeaux
56.48.03.44.

Michel Guérard
Eugénie-les-Bains
40320 Geaune
58.51.19.01.
Service until 10 pm.
Closed November 4–March 30.
Card: AE.

Hôtel de France
Place de la Libération
32000 Auch
65.05.00.44.
Service until 9:30 pm.
Closed Sunday evening,
Monday; January.
Cards: V, AE, DC, EC.

Les Pyrénées
19 pl. du Général-de-Gaulle
64220 Saint-Jean-
Pied-de-Port
59.37.01.01.
Service until 9 pm.
Closed Monday evening
(November–March),
Tuesday (exc. summer).
Cards: V, AE.

Jean Ramet
7-8 pl. Jean-Jaurès
33000 Bordeaux
56.44.12.51.
Service until 10 pm.
Closed Saturday, Sunday;
Easter week; August 10–24.
Card: V.

Saint-James
Jardins de Hauterive
3 pl. Camille-Hostein
Bouliac
33270 Floirac
56.20.52.19.
Service until 10 pm.
Open daily.
Cards: V, AE, DC.

La Tupina
6 rue Porte-de-la-Monnaie
33000 Bordeaux
56.91.56.37.
Service until 11 pm.
Closed Sunday.
Card: V.

Vanel
22 rue Maurice-Fonvielle
31000 Toulouse
61.21.51.82.
Service until 10 pm.
Closed Sunday,
Monday lunch; August.
Cards: AE, EC.

INDEX

175

The text was composed in ITC Century Expanded by
Datagraphic Services Inc., Valley Stream, New York.

The book was printed and bound by
Arnoldo Mondadori Editore S.p.A., Verona, Italy.